Securities Regulation

Fifth Edition

2007 Case Supplement

Aspen Publishers

2007 Case Supplement

Securities Regulation

Cases and Materials

Fifth Edition

James D. Cox
Brainerd Currie Professor of Law
Duke University

Robert W. Hillman
Professor of Law and Fair Business Practices Chair
University of California, Davis

Donald C. Langevoort
Thomas Aquinas Reynolds Professor of Law
Georgetown University

AUSTIN   BOSTON   CHICAGO   NEW YORK   THE NETHERLANDS

Aspen Publishers
Attn: Permissions Department
76 Ninth Avenue, 7th Floor
New York, NY 10011-5201

To contact Customer Care, e-mail customer.care@aspenpublishers.com, call 1-800-234-1660, fax 1-800-901-9075, or mail correspondence to:

Aspen Publishers
Attn: Order Department
PO Box 990
Frederick, MD 21705

Printed in the United States of America.

1 2 3 4 5 6 7 8 9 0

ISBN 978-0-7355-5770-3

Library of Congress Cataloguing-in-Publication Data

Cox, James D., 1943-
    Securities regulation: cases and materials / James D. Cox, Robert
W. Hillman, Donald C. Langevoort.– 5th ed.
    p. cm.
    Includes index.
    ISBN 0-7355-5960-0 (hardcover: alk. paper)
    1. Securities–United States–Cases. I. Hillman, Robert W. (Robert William), 1949- II. Langevoort, Donald C. III. Title.

    KF1438.C69 2006
    346.73'0922–dc22   2006000918

About Wolters Kluwer Law & Business

Wolters Kluwer Law & Business is a leading provider of research information and workflow solutions in key specialty areas. The strengths of the individual brands of Aspen Publishers, CCH, Kluwer Law International and Loislaw are aligned within Wolters Kluwer Law & Business to provide comprehensive, in-depth solutions and expert-authored content for the legal, professional and education markets.

CCH was founded in 1913 and has served more than four generations of business professionals and their clients. The CCH products in the Wolters Kluwer Law & Business group are highly regarded electronic and print resources for legal, securities, antitrust and trade regulation, government contracting, banking, pension, payroll, employment and labor, and healthcare reimbursement and compliance professionals.

Aspen Publishers is a leading information provider for attorneys, business professionals and law students. Written by preeminent authorities, Aspen products offer analytical and practical information in a range of specialty practice areas from securities law and intellectual property to mergers and acquisitions and pension/benefits. Aspen's trusted legal education resources provide professors and students with high-quality, up-to-date and effective resources for successful instruction and study in all areas of the law.

Kluwer Law International supplies the global business community with comprehensive English-language international legal information. Legal practitioners, corporate counsel and business executives around the world rely on the Kluwer Law International journals, loose-leafs, books and electronic products for authoritative information in many areas of international legal practice.

Loislaw is a premier provider of digitized legal content to small law firm practitioners of various specializations. Loislaw provides attorneys with the ability to quickly and efficiently find the necessary legal information they need, when and where they need it, by facilitating access to primary law as well as state-specific law, records, forms and treatises.

Wolters Kluwer Law & Business, a unit of Wolters Kluwer, is headquartered in New York and Riverwoods, Illinois. Wolters Kluwer is a leading multinational publisher and information services company.

Table of Contents

‖ 4 ‖

‖ 5 ‖

||6||

Secondary Distributions   15

||7||

Recapitalizations, Reorganizations, and Acquisitions   21

||9||

Liability Under the Securities Act   23

||11||

Inquiries into the Materiality of Information   27

||12||

Fraud in Connection with the Purchase or
Sale of a Security   31

‖13‖

‖14‖

‖15‖

‖16‖

‖18‖

Table of Cases

Securities Regulation

Fifth Edition

2007 Case Supplement

‖4‖
The Public Offering

J.   The International Public Offering

3.   How the Public Offering Is Regulated Elsewhere: Contrasting Approaches

Page 241.   Before subsection a, add the following.

‖ **Interim Report of the Committee on Capital Markets Regulation (December 2006)**

. . . A leading indicator of the competitiveness of U.S. public equity markets is the ability of the U.S. market to attract listings of foreign companies engaging in initial public offerings — so-called global IPOs. During the 1990s the number of foreign companies listed on the NYSE increased from 100 to almost 400. NASDAQ enjoyed similar fortunes, while the European exchanges, including London, lost market share. In the new millennium the trend seems to have reversed. After some lean years (between 2001 and 2003), this segment of the market is booming again. In 2005, 352 companies issued equity outside of their home market for the first time, raising a total of $92 billion. In just the first nine months of 2006, 230 companies raised $86 billion, substantially above the numbers in 1999 and close to the 2000 levels.

Figure I.6 [omitted] reports the percentage of these global IPOs that listed in the U.S. equity market. It shows that during 2000, one of every two dollars raised globally was raised in the United States, while, in 2005, approximately one in every 20 dollars was raised in the United States. Similarly, during the same period the percentage of global IPOs that chose to list in the United States declined from 37 percent to 10 percent. . . . Twenty-four of twenty-five of the largest IPOs in 2005 and nine of the ten largest IPOs in 2006 to date took place outside the United States. The two large IPOs in the United States during these two years were U.S. domiciled companies. Although IPOs within a given country can be cyclical, this U.S. capital market decline does not appear to be a statistical accident, but rather a sign of declining competitiveness of the U.S. markets. We can see this difference by focusing on where companies that were issuing internationally decided to place their first issuances when raising capital outside their home markets. . . . The loss of market share exists in both the high-tech and non-high-tech sectors. In 2000, 50 percent of the global IPOs by value (30 percent by number) were in high-tech sectors (telecommunications, computers, internet, and biotech). In 2005-2006, those percentages declined to less than half. However, dividing the global IPOs into high-tech and non-high-tech reveals that the loss in market share is present in both, albeit smaller in the high-tech sector. Hence, the overall drop is not due solely to changes in the sector composition of global IPOs. . . . Nor is the overall drop due to the loss of IPOs from emerging markets like China and Russia. Chinese companies may seek to list in Hong Kong because Hong Kong is part of China, or London may become the natural place for Russian companies because London has become a second home for Russian tycoons. However, even if one excludes from the pool of global IPOs those coming from China, India, and Russia (and it is not obvious why we should) the loss in market share is not much less severe: from 50 percent to 10 percent.

After more than a decade of declining market share, in the past three years, London has increased its share of the global IPO market from 5 percent to almost 25 percent. Furthermore, London has begun to attract a greater share of IPOs from U.S. domiciled companies. Starting in 2002, a small number of U.S. companies abandoned the U.S. equity markets to list in London. In the first nine months of 2006, 11 U.S. companies chose to list in London instead of in the United States, raising approximately $800 million. If one adds the IPO of closed-end private equity funds done by KKR and AP Alternative Assets in the Euronext market in Amsterdam, 23 percent of all the IPO funds raised by domestic U.S. companies have been raised outside the United States. . . . In 1996, global advisory and underwriting fees in the United States accounted for 58 percent of the total of $27 billion; by 2005, they were only 42 percent of $59.1 billion. The compound annual growth rate in underwriting fees for the United States was 4 percent as compared to 10 percent in Europe over the same period.

One possible reaction to the U.S. loss of global IPOs is to dismiss its importance to the U.S. economy. In 2000, 100 foreign companies were listing in the United States, raising $55 billion in capital. Last year only 34 foreign companies listed here, raising only $5 billion in capital. . . . The direct impact on the U.S. economy is small, albeit not trivial. A loss of $50 billion in fund raising implies a loss of at least $2.8 billion in underwriting fees and an annual loss of $3.3 billion in trading revenues. Because IPOs are very likely to raise more equity in subsequent years, one can estimate an additional loss in revenues of roughly a billion dollars. The real significance of this development is what it may indicate for the future loss of U.S. IPOs and trading revenue from foreign companies deciding to delist. As discussed below, these developments may not be materializing faster due to restrictions on U.S. and foreign companies leaving the U.S. market. If our capital markets prove unattractive, U.S. companies will demand the right to use cheaper foreign alternatives.

Some argue that the United States is well served by losing foreign IPOs, precisely because they pose unacceptable risks — for example, Chinese and Russian IPOs — to U.S. investors. The United States permits any company to issue stock in our market that makes the mandatory disclosures provided for in our registration requirements. The 1933 and 1934 Acts rejected "merit" regulation. In any event, our loss of foreign IPOs is even more severe when we restrict our attention to global IPOs from developed countries (Western Europe, Australia, Canada, Japan, and New Zealand), which may be less likely to pose these risks. . . .

A. BETTER REGULATED FOREIGN PUBLIC MARKETS

London's system of regulation has been completely reformed over the last 20 years. The "Big Bang" reforms instituted on October 27, 1986 modernized and liberalized the (briefly renamed) International Stock Exchange and ended the stagnation of the London equity market. Fixed commissions and restrictions on membership by commercial banks were eliminated, and traders moved from open-outcry to screen-based trading.

On May 20, 1997, the regulatory system established by the Financial Services Act of 1986 was again completely revamped. Until that date, the British system split responsibility between the Bank of England, the Securities and Investments Board (SIB), various Self-Regulatory Organizations (SROs), and a number of so-called Recognized Professional Bodies. This system was inefficient, confusing, and lacked a clear allocation of responsibility and accountability; moreover, it had failed to adequately protect investors. In 2000, a further consolidation resulted in the creation of the Financial Services Authority (FSA).

Sir Howard Davies, now Director of the London School of Economics and Political Science and former Chairman of the FSA, describes the establishment of the FSA as "the key step" in the United Kingdom's effort to secure London's financial leadership. The Financial Services and Markets Act (2000) brought not just the clarity and efficiency of a single regulator but a greatly increased degree of regulatory transparency and accountability. Among other things, the legislation requires the FSA to publish cost-benefit analyses of any proposed regulatory change, solicit comments on the proposal, and publish an account of its responses to those comments along with the final rule — that is, the FSA must explain itself if it takes action to which market participants object. The FSA also is subject to cost-effectiveness reviews by H.M. Treasury.

Even more important to the effectiveness of the FSA is the Authority's independence and the "market ownership of the system." First, by delegating expansive rulemaking power to the FSA and taking care not to give the appearance of interference (particularly regarding supervision issues affecting individual firms), the British government and its ministers have attempted to instill practitioners and consumers with confidence in the system. Furthermore, by taking over Listing Authority from the LSE in 2000, the FSA reduced duplication and separated the roles of market and regulation. In addition to ensuring the independence of the FSA, the Financial Services and Markets Act makes practitioners and consumers stakeholders in the Authority. Half of the Independent Directors of the FSA are from City firms. Moreover, the Financial Services and Markets Act establishes both practitioner and consumer panels to represent the interests of these constituencies. The practitioner panel has regular access to FSA staff, with which it consults regarding policy and regulatory initiatives. The FSA's decision to create separate divisions responsible for retail markets and institutional markets grew out of such a process. Finally, the FSA controls its own budget, based upon fees paid by market participants; thus, it can make improvements without demanding increased funding from the government.

In a November 2005 Oxera study, financial services professionals identified "regulatory environment" as the second most important determinant of financial center competitiveness (availability of skilled personnel was first). These practitioners preferred the regulatory environment of London to that of New York on two counts: first, practitioners felt that "there are too many regulatory bodies in USA and that there is a lack of consistency between them"; second, practitioners preferred the more flexible, principles-based regulatory philosophy adopted by the FSA to the prescriptive, rules-based approach of the SEC.

The Hong Kong securities regulatory environment also has improved substantially in recent years, although some still consider the regime too lax. According to studies by the International Institute for

Management Development ("IMD") and World Economic Forum ("WEF"), seven measures are identified as closely related to the regulatory environment and government responsiveness, as among them efficiency of legal framework, regulatory intensity, regulatory burden, and adaptability of government policies to economic changes. Among the 13 countries in Asia, the Chinese market in Hong Kong ranks very high on all measures.

Major regulatory changes have occurred during the last few years. In particular, the Securities and Futures Ordinance ("SFO"), which came into effect on April 1, 2003, was implemented to revamp Hong Kong securities regulation, by consolidating and modernizing ten existing ordinances into one composite piece of legislation. The SFO extended the Securities and Futures Commission's ("SFC") regulatory powers by bringing companies into the SFC's jurisdiction under a dual filing system where listed companies submit documents to both the exchange and the SFC, instead of solely the exchanges. The law also extended the SFC's powers to inspect and investigate companies and to impose sanctions. Other key provisions include establishing a market misconduct tribunal and improving an investor compensation fund that provides some relief to injured market participants.

||5||

Exempt Transactions

D. Regulation D and the Limited Offering Exemptions

2. Accredited Investors

Page 294.   Add the following new note after note 3.

4. Adjusting the Wealth Standard for Certain Private Offerings. The Commission has proposed new rules for accreditation standards that would apply to Regulation D and Section 4(6) offerings by a limited class of pooled investment funds (principally hedge funds) having fewer than 100 beneficial owners. *See* Release No. 33-8766. The proposals would add a new concept, the "accredited natural person," defined as a natural person who meets the existing net worth standards for an accredited investor ($1 million in assets or an income of $200,000) and also owns not less than $2.5 million in investments. The $2.5 million threshold will be adjusted every five years to account for inflation.

Although the proposed changes are limited to a small class of investment funds, they raise larger questions concerning the continuing relevance of a wealth standard for accreditation that has not been revisited since the adoption of Regulation D 25 years ago. Along this line, in proposing the new accreditation rules, the SEC has invited comment on the desirability of changes in the general standards for accredited investors under Regulation D and Section 4(6).

5. *Limitations on the Manner and Scope of an Offering*

g. *Is Reform Likely or Desirable?*

Page 312. **Add the following insert after the carryover paragraph at the top of the page.**

Final Report of the Advisory Committee on Smaller Public Companies to the U.S. Securities and Exchange Commission
(2006)

Recommendation IV.P.5:

> **Adopt a new private offering exemption from the registration require- ments of the Securities Act that does not prohibit general solicitation and advertising for transactions with purchasers who do not need all the protections of the Securities Act's registration requirements. Addition- ally, relax prohibitions against general solicitation and advertising found in Rule 502(c) under the Securities Act to parallel the "test the waters" model of Rule 254 under that Act.**

The ban on general solicitation and advertising in connection with exempt private offerings dates back to some of the earliest SEC staff interpretations of the Securities Act. Although the initial intention of the ban is straightforward, over time its application has become complex. Few bright-line tests exist, and issuers are required to make highly subjective determinations concerning whether their actions might be construed as impermissible. Among the factors the SEC staff has considered in determining if a general solicitation has occurred are: the number of offerees; their suitability as potential investors; how the offerees were contacted; and whether the offerees have a pre-existing business relationship with the issuer.

Beyond the difficulty of determining if particular contact is impermissible, however, the current ban on general solicitation and advertising effectively prohibits issuers from taking advantage of the tremendous efficiencies and reach of the Internet to communicate with potential investors who do not need all the protections of the Securities Act's registration requirements. In our view, this is a significant impediment to the efficient formation of capital for smaller companies, one that could easily be corrected by modernizing the existing prohibitions on advertising and general solicitation.

Traditionally, both federal and state private offering exemptions have been conditioned on the absence of "advertising or general solicitation." These concepts and SEC interpretations have not provided bright-line objective criteria for issuers and their advisers. Nevertheless, when it comes to exempt transactions, issuers face draconian risks to the viability of the entire offering for non-compliance with just one of the many required exemption elements. For example, even if all purchasers (A) are accredited investors, (B) have pre-existing business relationships with the issuing company and (C) are contacted in face-to-face meetings, some case law supports the view that the exemption will nevertheless be lost for the entire offering if other issuer activities are found to have involved general solicitation or advertising. . . . As a result, prudence dictates that the available methods used to contact offerees be very limited. In our view, concerns with avoiding improper general solicitation or advertising have the effect of focusing a disproportionate amount of time and effort on persons who may never purchase securities — rather than on the actual investors and their need for protection under the Securities Act.

Accordingly, we recommend the adoption of a new private offering exemption that would permit sales made only to certain eligible purchasers who do not require the full protections afforded by the securities registration process under the Securities Act because of (1) financial wherewithal, (2) investment sophistication, (3) relationship to the issuer or (4) institutional status. An offering whose purchasers consisted solely of eligible purchasers of these types would qualify for the exemption regardless of the means by which they were contacted — even through advertising or general solicitation activities, subject to the restrictions noted below.

- The class of eligible purchasers would be comprised of several categories of natural persons and legal entities and would be defined in a manner similar to that used in Regulation D under the Securities Act to define the term "accredited investors."
- Natural persons would qualify as eligible purchasers based on (1) wealth or annual income, (2) investment sophistication, (3) position with or relationship to the issuer (officer, director, key employee, existing significant stockholder, etc.) or (4) pre-existing business relationship with the issuer. Persons closely related to or associated with eligible purchasers would also qualify as eligible purchasers.
- The financial wherewithal standards for natural persons to qualify as eligible purchasers would be substantially higher than those

currently in effect for natural person Accredited Investors. We suggest $2 million in joint net worth or $300,000 in annual income for natural persons and $400,000 for joint annual income.

- Legal entities would qualify as eligible purchasers if they qualify as accredited investors under Regulation D.
- The SEC should adopt the new exemption amending Regulation D or adopt an entirely new amendment under Section 4(2) of the Securities Act, so that securities sold in reliance on the new exemption would be "covered securities" within the meaning of Section 18 of the Securities Act and generally exempted from the securities registration requirements of individual state securities laws. This course of action is crucial to the efficacy of the new exemption.
- The new exemption will need a two-way integration or aggregation safe harbor similar to that included in SEC Rule 701. Under such a safe harbor, offers and sales made in compliance with the new exemption would not be subject to integration or aggregation with offers and sales made under other exemptions or in registered offerings. Similarly, offers and sales made under other exemptions or in registered offerings would not be subject to integration or aggregation with transactions under the new exemption.
- As a means of guarding against potential abuse, we envision that all solicitations made by means of mass media (*e.g.*, newspapers, magazines, mass mailings or the Internet) would be restricted in scope to basic information about the issuer, similar to that found in Securities Act Rule 135c (currently a permissive rather than restrictive provision, and one applicable only to Exchange Act reporting companies). Solicitations made in face-to-face meetings would not be subject to these restrictions. . . .

The proposed exemption is not a radical change in the fundamental regulatory rationale regarding exempt private offerings. In all the private offerings since the beginning of regulatory time, no offeree has ever lost any money unless he or she became a purchaser. The new exemption reduces the issuer's obligations regarding non-investors and refocuses on the need (or lack thereof) that *actual purchasers* have for the protections afforded by the securities registration process. . . .

[I]n order to work effectively the new exemption will need to be implemented by adoption of a new or amended rule under Section 4(2) of the Securities Act, such that securities sold in reliance on the new exemption would be "covered securities" within the meaning of Section 18 of the Securities Act and consequently exempted from state securities registration requirements.

10

8. Additional Regulation D Requirements and Features

c. Integration of Offerings: The Safe Harbor

Page 318. Add the following at the end of the last full paragraph.

The 2006 Report of the Advisory Committee on Smaller Public Companies, Securities Act Release No. 8666, recommends shortening the integration safe harbor from 6 months to 30 days. The report reasons:

> The concept of integration . . . has been the subject of intense criticism, almost since its inception, and small business issuers and their legal advisors have long expressed concerns about the absence of clarity in being able to determine the circumstances under which integration does (or does not) apply. Though the SEC attempted to introduce more certainty into the determination by introduction of a five-factor test in 1961, as a practical matter the question of integration remains for smaller companies an area fraught with uncertainty — and therefore risk.
>
> Because of the link between integration and the availability of Regulation D and other registration exemptions, and consequently the ability of a smaller company to undertake a private financing, we believe that the SEC should provide smaller companies with clearer guidance concerning the circumstances under which two or more apparently separate offerings will or will not be integrated. After considering the difficulties of modifying the five-factor test in order to encompass the entire range of potential offering scenarios, we concluded that shortcomings of the existing framework can most easily be addressed by shortening the six-month safe harbor of Regulation D and applying the shortened safe harbor across the entire universe of private offering exemptions.
>
> The Regulation D safe harbor provides generally that offers and sales made more than six months before the start of a Regulation D offering or more than six months after completion of a Regulation D offering will not be considered part of that Regulation D offering. . . . Although it provides certainty, however, the safe harbor does so at the expense of flexibility, as it requires that as much as a full year elapse between offerings. For smaller companies, whose financing needs are often erratic and unpredictable, the duration of the safe harbor period is often problematic; even a well meaning issuer that needs access to capital, because of changed circumstances or greater than anticipated need for funding, may be unable to access such funds without running afoul of Section 5.
>
> Inasmuch as the alternative to the safe harbor is the inherent uncertainty of the five-factor test, the practical effect of the waiting period between Regulation D offerings is to undermine issuers' flexibility and impede them from obtaining financing at a time that business goals, and good judgment, would otherwise dictate. . . .

We believe that a shorter safe harbor period between offerings of 30 days strikes a more appropriate balance between the financing needs of smaller companies and investor protection, while preserving both investor protection and the integrity of the existing registration/exemption framework.

E. *Employee Benefit Plans and Contracts Relating to Compensation: Rule 701*

Page 323. Insert the following at the end of Release No. 33-7645 and before the Notes and Questions.

Final Report of the Advisory Committee on Smaller Public Companies to the U.S. Securities and Exchange Commission
(2006)

Recommendation IV.S.7:

Increase the disclosure threshold of Securities Act Rule 701(e) from $5 million to $20 million.

[O]ver time, Rule 701 has proved to be an extraordinarily useful exemption for both small businesses and large private companies, and for the most part continues to work well. Nonetheless, the disclosure of financial statement information has been problematic for growing companies in recent years as a result of the recent trend towards longer IPO incubation periods, particularly in a "down" market environment, as well as the increased use of equity awards as an incentive for attracting/ retaining employees. For private companies that hope to maintain the confidentiality of their financial information for competitive reasons, the increasing need for equity compensation presents a dilemma: disclose such information, and expose yourself to potential competitive harm (particularly relative to other private companies that are not required to disclose such information), or restrict equity awards to a limit below that which business conditions and sound judgment might otherwise dictate.

Based on the foregoing, we believe that an increase in the disclosure threshold of Rule 701(e) to $20 million represents a more appropriate balance between the informational needs of employee-investors and the confidentiality needs of private company issuers. The $5 million threshold was actually established in 1988, based upon the Commission's small issue exemptive limit at the time. The Committee's proposed increase would account for the amount of the original threshold that has been diminished due to inflation (as a point of reference, $5 million in 1988 would equal approximately $8.35 million today) as well as provide issuers with increased flexibility for granting equity awards without compromising confidentiality.

In the event that the Commission finds such increase in the disclosure threshold to be inadvisable, we recommend as an alternative that the financial statement disclosure requirements be eliminated or modified significantly if (1) options are non-transferable except by law and (2) options may only be exercised on a "net" basis with no employee funds paid to the issuer/employer.

G.   Integration of Offerings

Page 340.   Add the following update at the end of note 3.

The 2006 Report of the Advisory Committee on Smaller Public Companies, Securities Act Release No. 8666, recommends a clarification of the language of Rule 152 to permit a registered initial public offering to commence immediately after the completion of an otherwise valid private offering the stated purpose of which was to raise capital to fund an IPO. The Report notes:

> By its terms, the language of Rule 152 appears to require that an issuer "decide" to file for the public offering after the private offering. In other words, the safe harbor protection from integration would not appear to be available to an issuer that contemporaneously plans a private placement (for among other reasons, to raise funds necessary to sustain it through the IPO process) and a subsequent registered offering. Moreover, Rule 152 does not apply to private offerings undertaken pursuant to Rules 504 or 505, which are exempt pursuant to Securities Act Section 3(b), not Section 4(2) as set forth in the rule. Although the staff of the Division of Corporation Finance has indicated that it does not interpret Rule 152 literally, and will extend safe harbor treatment even in cases where an issuer concurrently plans a private placement and registered offering, we believe that it is time to clarify or amend the language of the rule appropriately.

|6|

Secondary Distributions

D. Rule 144 — Safe Harbor for Resales of Control and Restricted Securities

Page 372. Add the following before the Notes and Questions.

‖ Securities and Exchange Commission v. Kern
425 F.3d 143 (2d Cir. 2005)

POOLER, Circuit Judge.

[The SEC's enforcement action focused on a scheme involving three corporations, Polus, Inc., Citron, Inc., and Electronic Transfer Associates, Inc. (collectively "Issuers"). Each Issuer had been either incorporated or purchased variously by Richard Kern, Donald Kern, or Charles Wilkins (collectively "Sellers") and their shares were held by family and friends of their incorporator or purchaser (collectively "Owners"). In early 1998, Lybrand offered to purchase from Sellers 90 percent or more of each Issuer's shares for $150,000. This prompted Sellers to acquire the Owners' shares for extremely nominal consideration. Thereafter, also in 1998, Sellers caused the Issuers to effect ten-for-one stock splits and initiated through a broker a series of sales of the Issuer's shares that were matched with their purchase by Lybrand. The scheme of matched-order sales created a false appearance of investor interest in each Issuer's shares. Most of the shares that were not subject to the matched orders were transferred to entities controlled by Lybrand, but about 5% were retained by Sellers. The background leading up to the resales of Electronic

Transfer Associates, Inc. (ETA) shares was slightly different because Richard Kern and his spouse held 75 percent of the ETA shares so that most of the shares resold by Lybrand could be traced to this block of shares. By 1999, the matched orders for Issuers' shares had their intended effect of boosting the shares' values. Sellers then sold their remaining shares, i.e., the shares not sold to Lybrand, in the over-the-counter market, netting about $6 million in profits. The district court held that the defendants' sales were not exempt under Section 4(1); hence, they violated Section 5 and were ordered to disgorge their profits and incur civil penalties of $1.1 million.]

I. STATUTORY AND REGULATORY REGIME

Section 5 of the Act provides that securities must be registered with the Commission before any person may sell or offer to sell such securities. . . . Section 4 of the Act creates a number of exemptions from this general rule. Id. . . . The exemption primarily at issue in this case is found in Section 4(1), which exempts "transactions by any person other than an issuer, underwriter, or dealer." Id. . . . An underwriter is defined in relevant part in Section 2(a)(11) as "any person who has purchased from an issuer with a view to, or offers or sells for an issuer in connection with, the distribution of any security, or participates or has a direct or indirect participation in any such undertaking, or participates or has a participation in the direct or indirect underwriting of any such undertaking." Id. . . .). For purposes of the underwriter definition only, an issuer includes any person controlling, controlled by, or under common control with the issuer of the securities. Id. In light of the purpose of the Act, exemptions generally are to be interpreted to promote full disclosure of information necessary to protect the investing public. *SEC v. Ralston Purina Co., 346 U.S. 119 . . . (1953).*

In order to provide greater certainty and security to issuers and investors, the Commission has limited the definition of "underwriter" to exclude any person who meets the requirements of the Rule 144 safe harbor. Id. . . . This consequence is precisely limited to its terms. A person who fails to comply with Rule 144 does not benefit from the safe harbor, but can still avoid underwriter status if he does not meet the statutory definition of an underwriter. Id. . . . Similarly, a person who complies with Rule 144 must still show that he is neither an issuer nor a dealer to qualify for the 4(1) exemption. . . .

To comply with Rule 144, a person ordinarily must meet numerous requirements concerning public information, holding periods, number of shares, manner of sales, and notice to the Commission. Id. . . . However, under subsection (k) of the Rule, if a person is not now and has not been an affiliate of the issuer within the last three months, and at least two years have elapsed since the securities to be sold were last acquired from an issuer or affiliate of the issuer, then that person need not comply with the other Rule 144 requirements. Id. . . . An "affiliate" is in turn defined as "a person that directly, or indirectly . . . controls, or is controlled by, or is under common control with [the] issuer." Id. . . .

It is undisputed that none of the securities sold here were registered. To avoid liability, the Sellers must therefore demonstrate that they qualify for an exemption from the registration requirement of Section 5. On appeal, the Sellers argue only that the Polus and Citron transactions were exempt under Rule 144(k), and that the ETA transactions were exempt under Section 4(1). Furthermore, appellants argue on appeal only the legality of the January and February 1999 sales, which essentially correspond to the Market Sales. We therefore take it as conceded that the pre-1999 sales were illegal, that all defendants-appellants are liable if all the Sellers are liable, that the Polus and Citron transactions are exempt under Section 4(1) only if they qualify for the Rule 144 safe harbor under subsection (k), and that the ETA transactions are not protected by Rule 144 at all.

II.   Polus and Citron: Rule 144(k) . . .

A.   Affiliate Status of the Owners . . .

Rule 144(k) requires, in part, that "a period of at least two years has elapsed since the later of the date the securities [at issue] were acquired from the issuer or from an affiliate of the issuer. Rule 144 defines " 'affiliate' of an issuer" as any "person that directly, or indirectly through one or more intermediaries, controls, or is controlled by, or is under common control with, such issuer." Id. . . . While Rule 144 fails to define "control," Rule 405 of Regulation C establishes a definition of "affiliate" identical to that of Rule 144 and defines "control" . . .

Here, there is no serious dispute that Sellers dominated Citron and Polus up until only a few months prior to the January and February 1999 Market Sales at issue. The Sellers dominated the limited affairs pertinent to each company and orchestrated the transfer of the shells to Lybrand by agreements reached between May and June of 1998. As noted, Polus and Citron were blank-check companies. Richard Kern had founded Citron, served as its president, and served as one of only two directors, along with his wife. After founding the company, Kern distributed most of the shares in Citron to the Owners. Wilkins had "purchased 98 percent of the

17

outstanding . . . stock of Polus in July 1996" and distributed stock to the Owners. During this period, the companies observed no corporate formalities. Together, the Sellers possessed and exercised the power to direct the management of Citron and Polus by the domination of the limited affairs and transfer of the companies.

During the same period of time, Sellers also controlled the Owners. Because of this control—part of a joint scheme to acquire and transfer stock to Lybrand for distribution—the Owners were under common control with Citron and Polus by Sellers so that two years had not passed since the stock of those issuers was held by non-affiliates when Sellers executed the Market Sales in early 1999. Therefore, 144(k)'s safe harbor is unavailable to defendants. Sellers claim that any actual control exercised over Owners by them was insufficient to establish Owners' affiliate status because "legal control is required to satisfy" the definition of an affiliate. . . . Under the language of Rules 144(a)(1) and 405, this argument fails. . . .

Rule 405, by its language, refers to control broadly as "the possession, direct or indirect, of the power to direct or cause the direction of the management and policies of a person whether through ownership of voting securities, contract, or otherwise." . . . This broad language supports a "control" conclusion, where, as here, the controlling persons so dominated those controlled as to be able to gain upwards of 90% of the stock from Owners who were in a relationship of trust with Sellers. Indeed, this transaction—attempting to garner large quantities of closely held companies' stock in anticipation of public distribution—is exactly the type of transaction for which the Act was intended to require disclosure. . . . The proof of control over Owners here rests in the ability of Sellers to garner overwhelming proportions of Citron and Polus' stock at a fraction of the price at which it was sold to Lybrand for distribution.

We therefore conclude that the Owners and the Issuers were under the common control of the Sellers at the time that the Sellers acquired shares from the Owners. As a result, these acquisitions were from affiliates of the Issuers within two years of the sales, and the Sellers are thereby disqualified from Rule 144(k) protection.

B. IDENTITY BETWEEN OWNERS AND SELLERS

[The Sellers raised two arguments, each premised upon the close relationship between the Sellers and the Owners that prevented their being considered underwriters. First, they argued that because of the close relationship they should be viewed collectively as the same "person" so that the Sellers' acquisition of shares from the Owners should be seen as a nonevent. The court rejected this argument, reasoning that the relevance of the definition of "person" in Rule 144(a)(2) is to determine for whose account the securities are being sold. Thus, even if the Sellers and Owners were a single person the shares' sale would be for the account of the Sellers.

The Sellers also argued that because Sellers and Owners were so closely related the holding period of the Owners should be tacked to that of the Sellers so that the two-year holding period of Rule 144(k) would be met. The court recognized that Rule 144(d) identifies limited instances when the holding period can be tacked, e.g., the donee may tack the holding period of the donor and similarly the pledgee may tack the holding period of the pledgor. However, the court dismissed the argument, reasoning that tacking worked only in one direction and to succeed in this argument the Sellers would have to show that they were acting in the interests of the Owners so as to stand in their shoes. It believed the facts were to the contrary.]

We therefore conclude that the Sellers' creative objections are without merit, and do not affect our conclusion that the Polus and Citron sales are not exempted from registration under Rule 144(k). As a result, we need not reach the Commission's argument that Rule 144 will not protect any sale that is part of a scheme intended to effect a public distribution without registration.

III. ETA: Section 4(1)

We now consider whether the ETA sales, which concededly do not qualify for the Rule 144 safe harbor, are nonetheless exempt under Section 4(1). Although Rule 144 was intended to provide a safe harbor, it is clear that a person who does not comply with Rule 144 may still take advantage of the statutory terms of Section 4(1). . . . Section 2(a)(11) defines an "underwriter" as any person who purchases with a view to distribution, offers or sells for an issuer in connection with a distribution, or participates in any distribution or underwriting. . . . For purposes of this definition only, an "issuer" is defined to include the same control persons as would be termed "affiliates" under Rule 144. . . .

Because Kern and his wife had first obtained their 75% ownership of ETA in 1996 and held it until 1998, Kern argues that he could not have obtained these shares with a view to distribution. As to the 25% of shares acquired from the Owners, Kern argues that the identity of interests makes these acquisitions non-events for purposes of the statute. Finally, Kern also argues that his sales were for his own benefit, not the issuer's, so that he was not an underwriter under Section 2(a)(11). . . .

Section 4(1) exempts "transactions by any person other than an issuer, underwriter or dealer." . . . Thus, if any person involved in a transaction is a statutory underwriter, then none of the persons involved may claim exemption under Section 4(1). *See United States v. Wolfson, 405 F.2d 779, 782* (holding that where control persons sold securities through brokers, control persons could not claim exemption because brokers were underwriters under Section 2(a)(11)). Underwriters, in turn, include any person who is "engaged in steps necessary to the distribution of security issues." *Securities & Exchange Com. v. Chinese Consol. Benevolent Ass'n, 120 F.2d 738, 741 (2d Cir. 1941).*

There is no question that the 1998 sales involved underwriters; indeed, this has been effectively conceded by the Sellers' failure to argue that the 1998 sales did not violate Section 5. Even ignoring this concession, the profitability of Lybrand's scheme was based on the sale of securities to the public once the price had been manipulated upwards, so that the entities controlled by Lybrand acquired securities from affiliates with a view to distribution, and were therefore underwriters. As a result, the entire "transaction" is placed outside the Section 4(1) exemption.

The question, therefore, is whether the 1999 Market Sales were part of the same "transaction" as the 1998 Matched-Order Sales and Transfers for purposes of the Section 4(1) exemption. We conclude that they were. The Commission has described a distribution as continuing throughout "the entire process by which in the course of a public offering the block of securities is dispersed and ultimately comes to rest in the hands of the investing public." *R.A. Holman & Co., Inc. v. SEC, 366 F.2d 446, 449 (2d Cir. 1966)* (quoting *Lewisohn Copper Corp., 38 S.E.C. 226, 234 (1958)*). The fact that at some point in the midst of the transfer of ETA shares to the public, Kern ceased to be an affiliate, does not permit his remaining sales to become exempt under Section 4(1). Cutting off liability partway through a distribution by a control person would permit a control person to retain some fraction of the profits from such a distribution, thereby encouraging sales made without proper disclosures — precisely the result that *Ralston Purina* instructs us to avoid in interpreting exemptions. . . .

We therefore conclude that as a matter of law, the 1999 Market Sales are part of the same "transaction" as the 1998 sales. Because the earlier sales undisputedly involved underwriters, the entire offering is not exempt under Section 4(1). Summary judgment was therefore properly granted as to the ETA transactions. . . .

CONCLUSION

For the foregoing reasons, the judgment of the district court is affirmed.

||7||

Recapitalizations, Reorganizations, and Acquisitions

A. The "For Value" Requirement

2. Shells and Spin-offs: Creating "Value"

a. Spin-offs and the '33 Act

Page 405. Add the following new note after note 2.

3. Spin-offs and the Imaginative Use of Form S-8. Another route some promoters have employed to take a company public through the back door, i.e., without registration, is the artful use of Form S-8. Form S-8 is an abbreviated registration statement that is available to register securities offered exclusively to the issuers' employees and even its consultants. Because the purchasers are essentially insiders, the information required to be disclosed on Form S-8 is minimal. Abuses in the use of Form S-8 arose by promoters of shell companies registering shares of the shell company on Form S-8, issuing the shares to themselves and other "employees" and "consultants," and then acquiring a private company. Thereafter the shares registered on Form S-8 would be dumped on the public with no information about the issuer in either its '33 Act or '34 Act reports. To correct this problem, the SEC bars the use of Form S-8 by shell companies (defined as entities with no or nominal assets, or assets consisting solely of cash, or some combination of cash and nominal assets). As further protection to investors, Form 8-K now requires filing of information by a shell company bearing on a transaction that causes it to cease being a shell company. Excluded from the definition of shell company is an entity created specifically to facilitate reincorporation or an acquisition by an operating company. *See* Securities Act Rel. No. 8587 (June 29, 2005).

|9|

Liability Under the Securities Act

C. Section 12(a)(2)

1. By Means of a "Prospectus or Oral Communication"

Page 529. Add immediately after the *Gustafson* opinion and before the Notes and Questions.

‖ **Yung v. Lee**
‖ 432 F.3d 142 (2d Cir. 2006)

REENA RAGGI, Circuit Judge:

Plaintiffs Billy Yung and Yung Yau purchased securities offered privately by Integrated Transportation Network Group, Inc. ("ITNG"). . . . They now appeal from a judgment of the [district court] dismissing federal claims brought under Sections 12(a)(2) and 15 of the Securities Act of 1933. . . . Because we conclude that Section 12(a)(2) of the Securities Act does not afford a cause of action to persons, such as the plaintiffs, who purchased securities in a private offering and, therefore, not "by means of a prospectus," we hereby affirm the district court's dismissal of that statutory claim. . . .

I. BACKGROUND

[Defendant ITNG is a Delaware corporation with offices in New York. ITNG's shares were publicly listed and traded on the securities markets of the United States.

Defendant BDO Seidman, LLP, served as ITNG's principal independent auditor and accounting firm.]

Plaintiffs purchased their ITNG holdings directly from ITNG pursuant to a series of private subscription and letter agreements between December 17, 1998, and March 26, 1999. ITNG's solicitation of plaintiffs' purchases began on November 5, 1998, when ITNG representatives first met with Billy Yung, and continued during two subsequent meetings in November and a final meeting in December attended by defendant Andrew Lee. Each of these meetings was held in China, the first and third in Shenzhen, the second and fourth in Hong Kong. During these meetings, ITNG representatives presented the company's business plan and stressed an expected expansion in the Chinese market for auto leasing. ITNG also stressed the value of its taxi licenses, which was verified by the audited financial statements accompanying the plan. . . .

[E]ach subscription or letter agreement entered into by the plaintiffs stated, inter alia, that the securities "were being sold to the undersigned without registration under any state, or federal or PRC law requiring registration of securities for sale and accordingly will constitute 'restricted securities' as defined in Rule 144 of the U.S. Securities and Exchange Commission."

Plaintiffs assert that, in May 1999, they discovered that ITNG's financial position was "dire" because of previously undisclosed liabilities and "major problems" associated with ITNG's transportation businesses and properties in China. They submit that there were numerous false and misleading statements and omissions in [an earlier registration statement] and in the other publicly filed documents provided to them by defendants, which effectively concealed ITNG's true financial position at the time of the plaintiffs' purchases. . . .

II. DISCUSSION

[W]e hold that Section 12(a)(2) of the Securities Act does not apply to private transactions because such transactions are not subject to the prospectus delivery requirements of the Act as construed by the Supreme Court in Gustafson v. Alloyd Co., 513 U.S. 561, 115 S. Ct. 1061, 131 L. Ed. 2d 1 (1995). . . .

[P]laintiffs submit that they are entitled to sue BDO Seidman under this section because, although they purchased ITNG shares in a private rather than public offering, their purchases were made in reliance on a prospectus prepared for a public offering. Like the district court, we conclude that a Section 12(a)(2) claim cannot be maintained by a private purchaser of securities.

1.   Section 12(a)(2) Applies Only to Public Offerings of Securities

In Gustafson v. Alloyd Co., the Supreme Court considered whether the protections of Section 12(a)(2) "extend[] to a private, secondary transaction, on the theory that recitations in the purchase agreement are part of a 'prospectus.'" Before *Gustafson,* this court, and a number of our sister circuits, had ruled that Section 12(a)(2) "applies to private as well as public offerings of securities." . . . In *Gustafson,* however, the Supreme Court held that the plaintiffs could not sue under Section 12(a)(2) because their private sales contract did not qualify as a "prospectus." The Court explained that Section 12(a)(2) liability "cannot attach unless there is an obligation to distribute the prospectus in the first place (or unless there is an exemption)."[6] . . .

Gustafson's narrow construction of the term "prospectus" as used in Section 12(a)(2) has drawn sharp criticism. . . . No matter; the Supreme Court's interpretation of a statute binds lower federal courts in their application of that statute.

Thus far, this court has not had to reach the issue of whether the rationale for decision in *Gustafson,* which involved a private secondary sale, necessarily precludes a Section 12(a)(2) claim with respect to any private securities transaction. . . . Nevertheless, district courts in this circuit have routinely cited *Gustafson* in reaching what can reasonably be characterized as "the predominate conclusion that purchasers in private or secondary market offerings are precluded from bringing actions under Section 12(a)(2)." . . . Three of our sister circuits have considered the question and similarly concluded that a Section 12(a)(2) claim cannot be brought in connection with a private offering. . . .

We now join these courts in holding that *Gustafson's* definition of a prospectus as "a document that describes a public offering of securities" compels the conclusion that a Section 12(a)(2) action cannot be maintained by a plaintiff who acquires securities through a private transaction, whether primary or secondary. . . . A private offering is not

---

6.   Section 3 of the Securities Act exempts certain types of securities from the registration requirements of that statute. . . . Because the parties in this case do not argue that the securities at issue are exempt under Section 3, we need not consider this possibility.

effected "by means of a prospectus" because *Gustafson* states that Section 12(a)(2) liability cannot attach unless there is an "obligation to distribute a prospectus," 513 U.S. at 571, and there is no "obligation" to distribute a document that describes a public offering to a private purchaser.

2.   The Distribution of a Prospectus Prepared in Connection with a Public Offering to a Purchaser in a Private Transaction Does Not Permit that Purchaser to Pursue a Section 12(a)(2) Claim

Plaintiffs acknowledge that they purchased the securities at issue through a series of private transactions, not any public offering. . . . Nevertheless, plaintiffs argue on appeal . . . that they state a claim under Section 12(a)(2) because "the defendants' marketing of the ITNG shares relied heavily upon a recent company Registration Statement. . . . " Like the district court, we think that this construction of Section 12(a)(2) cannot easily be reconciled with the Supreme Court's reasoning in *Gustafson*.

The defendants were under no "obligation to distribute" the [prospectus used in the earlier registered offering] or any other prospectus to the plaintiffs in connection with the challenged private transactions. *Gustafson* indicates that without such an obligation, a securities transaction cannot reasonably be deemed to have occurred "by means of a prospectus." Gustafson v. Alloyd Co., 513 U.S. at 571 ("The liability imposed by § 12(a)(2) cannot attach unless there is an obligation to distribute the prospectus in the first place (or unless there is an exemption).").

In any event, under the express terms of the subscription and letter agreements, the parties agreed that the ITNG securities at issue "were not offered . . . by means of publicly disseminated advertisements or sales literature." . . . Where, as in this case, plaintiffs were aware at the time they signed this disclaimer that they had reviewed a prospectus disseminated in connection with a separate public offering, they will not be permitted to disavow this contract term to claim that the challenged offering was "by means of" the prospectus. . . .

III.   Conclusion

Because ITNG offered and sold securities to plaintiffs through private transactions, it was under no "obligation" to distribute any prospectus. Thus, it cannot be deemed to have sold securities "by means of a prospectus," as the term "prospectus" has been construed by the Supreme Court in *Gustafson*. . . .

‖11‖
Inquiries into the Materiality of Information

E. The SEC and Corporate Governance

2. The Interface of Materiality and Corporate Governance

Page 642. Substitute the following for current note 3.

3. Disclosure of Executive Compensation. In 2006, the SEC amended Item 402 of Regulation S-K to significantly expand the disclosure requirements for executive compensation. The SEC's action reflected the growing public malaise regarding both the level of executive compensation and the pace by which executive compensation has grown. Indeed, statistics reflect that only Major League Baseball and NBA players exceed the rate of growth executives have enjoyed in their compensation.

In broad overview, the new rules are divided in five primary areas:

1. Addition of a "Compensation Discussion and Analysis" ("CD&A") section to SEC filings and a new Compensation Committee Report.
2. Detailed disclosure of compensation for "named executive officers" ("NEOs") for the last fiscal year and the two preceding fiscal years.
3. Extensive disclosure of grants, holdings, and realization of equity-related interests (e.g., stock options, stock appreciation rights) to NEOs.
4. Retirement plans, deferred compensation, and other post-employment payments and benefits for NEOs.
5. Director compensation.

CD&A is a central component of the new disclosure requirements. The rules for this new part of SEC filings is principles based, meaning Item 402 broadly calls for registrants to set forth in a comprehensive way the material factors underlying the company's executive compensation policies and practices (instead of setting forth narrow categories of information that is to be provided). Areas of policy to be addressed include what are the objectives of the company's compensation program, what is sought to be rewarded by the compensation, the elements of the executive's compensation, how did the company determine the amount for each such element, and how does each element fit with the company's overall compensation objectives. The CD&A is also part of the CEO's and CFO's certification requirements.

The Compensation Committee Report must address two items: first, whether the committee has reviewed and discussed the CD&A; and, second, based on any review and discussion, the committee has recommended to the board that the CD&A be included in the company's SEC Filing. What appears to be the disclosure objective served by the Compensation Committee Report?

NEOs are the firm's principal executive officer (e.g., CEO) and principal financial officer (e.g., CFO) plus the other three most highly compensated officers (provided the person's compensation exceeds $100,000).

Executive compensation for NEOs is to be disclosed in a tabular format with the following set forth in separate columns: salary, bonus, dollar value of stock awards, dollar value of option awards, nonequity incentive plan compensation earned during the year, annual change in actuarial value of accumulated pension benefits, aggregate amount of all other compensation, including perquisites, and total compensation.

Also introduced in 2006 was expansion of the disclosures called for by Item 404 of Regulation S-K pertaining to related-party transactions. The new rules now require companies to describe their policies, procedures, and standards to be applied when there is a related-party transaction (now defined as transactions with certain company personnel involving at least $120,000).

Page 643. Insert the following after current note 3.

4. Corporate Governance Disclosure Requirements of Regulation S-K. In 2006, the SEC adopted Item 407 of Regulation S-K that consolidates various disclosure requirements related to director independence and corporate governance. Item 407 requires companies to disclose whether (and why) each director and director nominee is independent and whether any audit, nominating, or compensation committee member is not independent pursuant to any applicable listing standard (or a chosen standard if one does not apply). Companies that have adopted definitions of independence for directors either must set forth the definition or disclose if they appear on its web site. Specific disclosure is required of the compensation committee's governance structure, such as its processes and procedures for considering reaching compensation decisions including the involvement of executive officers and compensation consultants in setting compensation. Disclosures of whether and why a member of the audit committee can be considered a financial expert are now covered by Item 407.

||12||

Fraud in Connection with the Purchase or Sale of a Security

C. *Scienter:* **Hochfelder** *and Beyond*

2. **Pleading Scienter**

Page 680.   Insert the following at the end of note 1.

The Supreme Court granted certiorari in late 2006 in the case of *Makor Issues & Rights Ltd. v. Tellabs, Inc.*, 437 F.3d 588 (7th Cir. 2006). This was a fairly standard fraud-on-the-market action against Tellabs and certain of its executives, including its CEO, Nottebaert, for false and misleading statements in January through March of 2001 indicating that demand was strong for its core product (the TITAN 5500), that second quarter sales were expected to be in the $780-820 million range, and that a new generation product was immediately ready for shipment. In June, the company acknowledged that second quarter revenues would only be $500 million because of an enormous reduction in sales of the TITAN 5500. At no time during the class period, moreover, was the new generation product ever ready for sale.

The district court dismissed the case as against Nottebaert for failure to create a strong inference of scienter. The Seventh Circuit reversed. With respect to the heightened pleading standard for scienter, the court aligned itself with the middle ground approach of other circuits (e.g., *Greebel,* supra) that take all the facts and circumstances into account. The most striking portion of the holding was that if the facts alleged in the pleadings admit of multiple plausible inferences — some consistent with scienter, others not — the case should not be dismissed. The court went so far as to suggest that the Seventh Amendment's right to a jury trial might be infringed otherwise. It rejected the standard prevailing in other circuits that allows plaintiffs to go forward to discovery only if the most plausible of the competing inferences indicates that the defendant acted with scienter. Instead, it is enough that a reasonable person could infer scienter from the facts set forth in the complaint. Having thus set the pleading standard relatively low, the court determined that the pleadings against Nottebaert were sufficient: There were allegations that he was well in the loop in early 2001 when internal reports were showing the reduction in sales and the new product's lack of readiness, even though there was no direct evidence of his actual knowledge.

The SEC and Department of Justice filed an *amicus* brief before the Supreme Court urging reversal. The government's brief argued that the Seventh Circuit's approach of letting the case go forward so long as scienter is *a* permissible inference contravenes the plain language of the statute, which insists on a *strong* inference, and that the court's approach was essentially what many courts had been doing before the PSLRA was adopted — precisely what Congress sought to overturn. The brief suggests that the right standard is "whether, taking the alleged facts as true, there is a *high likelihood* that the conclusion that the defendant possessed scienter follows from those facts." *Brief for the United States*, at 8 (emphasis added).

‖13‖

The Enforcement of the Securities Laws

A. More on the Private Enforcement of the Securities Laws

1. Champion of the Little Guy: The Class Action

c. Closing the Bypass: The Securities Litigation Uniform Standards Act

‖ **Merrill Lynch, Pierce, Fenner & Smith, Inc. v. Dabit**
‖ **126 S. Ct. 1503 (2006)**

Justice STEVENS delivered the opinion of the Court.

Title I of the Securities Litigation Uniform Standards Act of 1998 (SLUSA) provides that "[n]o covered class action" based on state law and alleging "a misrepresentation or omission of a material fact in connection with the purchase or sale of a covered security" "may be maintained in any State or Federal court by any private party." §101(b), 112 Stat. 3227 (codified at *15 U.S.C. §78bb(f)(1)(A)*). In this case the Second Circuit held that SLUSA only pre-empts state-law class-action claims brought by plaintiffs who have a private remedy under federal law. *395 F.3d 25 (2005)*. A few months later, the Seventh Circuit ruled to the contrary, holding that the statute also pre-empts state-law class-action claims for which federal law provides no private remedy. *Kircher v. Putnam Funds Trust, 403 F.3d 478 (2005)*. The background, the text, and the purpose of SLUSA's pre-emption provision all support the broader interpretation adopted by the Seventh Circuit.

I.

Petitioner Merrill Lynch, Pierce, Fenner & Smith, Inc. (Merrill Lynch), is an investment banking firm that offers research and brokerage services to investors. Suspicious that the firm's loyalties to its investment banking clients had produced biased investment advice, the New York attorney general in 2002 instituted a formal investigation into Merrill Lynch's practices. The investigation sparked a number of private securities fraud actions, this one among them.

Respondent, Shadi Dabit, is a former Merrill Lynch broker. He filed this class action in the United States District Court for the Western District of Oklahoma on behalf of himself and all other former or current brokers who, while employed by Merrill Lynch, purchased (for themselves and for their clients) certain stocks between December 1, 1999, and December 31, 2000. . . . Rather than rely on the federal securities laws, Dabit invoked the District Court's diversity jurisdiction and advanced his claims under Oklahoma state law.

The gist of Dabit's complaint was that Merrill Lynch breached the fiduciary duty and covenant of good faith and fair dealing it owed its brokers by disseminating misleading research and thereby manipulating stock prices. Dabit's theory was that Merrill Lynch used its misinformed brokers to enhance the prices of its investment banking clients' stocks: The research analysts, under management's direction, allegedly issued overly optimistic appraisals of the stocks' value; the brokers allegedly relied on the analysts' reports in advising their investor clients and in deciding whether or not to sell their own holdings; and the clients and brokers both continued to hold their stocks long beyond the point when, had the truth been known, they would have sold. The complaint further alleged that when the truth was actually revealed (around the time the New York attorney general instituted his investigation), the stocks' prices plummeted.

Dabit asserted that Merrill Lynch's actions damaged the class members in two ways: The misrepresentations and manipulative tactics caused them to hold onto overvalued securities, and the brokers lost commission fees when their clients, now aware that they had made poor investments, took their business elsewhere. . . .

[D]ozens of other suits, based on allegations similar to Dabit's, . . . [were] filed against Merrill Lynch around the country on both federal- and state-law theories of liability. The Judicial Panel on Multidistrict Litigation transferred all of those cases, along with this one, to the United States District Court for the Southern District of New York for consolidated pretrial proceedings. Merrill Lynch then filed its second motion to dismiss Dabit's complaint. Senior Judge Milton Pollack granted the motion on the ground that the claims alleged fell "squarely within SLUSA's ambit." *Ciccarelli v. Merrill Lynch & Co. (In re Merrill Lynch & Co.*

*Research Reports Sec. Litig.), 2003 U.S. Dist. LEXIS 5999, 2003 WL 1872820, *1 (Apr. 10, 2003).*

The Court of Appeals for the Second Circuit, however, vacated the judgment and remanded for further proceedings. *395 F.3d at 51.* It concluded that the claims asserted by holders did not allege fraud "in connection with the purchase or sale" of securities under SLUSA. Although the court agreed with Merrill Lynch that that phrase, as used in other federal securities laws, has been defined broadly by this Court, it held that Congress nonetheless intended a narrower meaning here — one that incorporates the "standing" limitation on private federal securities actions adopted in *Blue Chip Stamps v. Manor Drug Stores, 421 U.S. 723 . . . (1975).* Under the Second Circuit's analysis, fraud is only "in connection with the purchase or sale" of securities, as used in SLUSA, if it is alleged by a purchaser or seller of securities. Thus, to the extent that the complaint in this action alleged that brokers were fraudulently induced, not to sell or purchase, but to retain or delay selling their securities, it fell outside SLUSA's pre-emptive scope.[3] . . .

For the reasons that follow, we disagree. . . .

IV.

The core provision of SLUSA reads as follows:

> "Class Action Limitations. — No covered class action based upon the statutory or common law of any State or subdivision thereof may be maintained in any State or Federal court by any private party alleging —
> "(A) a misrepresentation or omission of a material fact in connection with the purchase or sale of a covered security; or
> "(B) that the defendant used or employed any manipulative or deceptive device or contrivance in connection with the purchase or sale of a covered security." Id., at 3230 (codified as amended at *15 U.S.C. §78bb(f)(1)).*[7]

A "covered class action" is a lawsuit in which damages are sought on behalf of more than 50 people. A "covered security" is one traded nationally and listed on a regulated national exchange. Respondent does

---

3. The Court of Appeals also concluded that Dabit's lost commission claims escaped pre-emption under SLUSA because they did not "allege fraud that 'coincide[s]' with the sale or purchase of a security." *395 F.3d at 47* (quoting *SEC v. Zandford, 535 U.S. 813, 825, 122 S. Ct. 1899, 153 L. Ed. 2d 1 (2002)).* That determination is not before this Court for review.

7. Another key provision of the statute makes all "covered class actions" filed in state court removable to federal court. 112 Stat. 3230 (codified at *15 U.S.C. §78bb(f)(2)).*

not dispute that both the class and the securities at issue in this case are "covered" within the meaning of the statute, or that the complaint alleges misrepresentations and omissions of material facts. The only disputed issue is whether the alleged wrongdoing was "in connection with the purchase or sale" of securities.

Respondent urges that the operative language must be read narrowly to encompass (and therefore pre-empt) only those actions in which the purchaser-seller requirement of *Blue Chip Stamps* is met. Such, too, was the Second Circuit's view. But insofar as the argument assumes that the rule adopted in *Blue Chip Stamps* stems from the text of *Rule 10b-5* — specifically, the "in connection with" language, it must be rejected. Unlike the *Birnbaum* court, which relied on *Rule 10b-5*'s text in crafting its purchaser-seller limitation, this Court in *Blue Chip Stamps* relied chiefly, and candidly, on "policy considerations" in adopting that limitation. *421 U.S., at 737. . . .* The *Blue Chip Stamps* Court purported to define the scope of a private right of action under *Rule 10b-5* — not to define the words "in connection with the purchase or sale." Id., *at 749. . . .*

Congress can hardly have been unaware of the broad construction adopted by both this Court and the SEC when it imported the key phrase — "in connection with the purchase or sale" — into SLUSA's core provision. And when "judicial interpretations have settled the meaning of an existing statutory provision, repetition of the same language in a new statute indicates, as a general matter, the intent to incorporate its . . . judicial interpretations as well." *Bragdon v. Abbott, 524 U.S. 624, 645 . . . (1998) . . .* Application of that presumption is particularly apt here; not only did Congress use the same words as are used in *§10(b)* and *Rule 10b-5*, but it used them in a provision that appears in the same statute as *§10(b)*. Generally, "identical words used in different parts of the same statute are . . . presumed to have the same meaning." *IBP, Inc. v. Alvarez, 546 U.S. 1144. . . .*

The presumption that Congress envisioned a broad construction follows not only from ordinary principles of statutory construction but also from the particular concerns that culminated in SLUSA's enactment. A narrow reading of the statute would undercut the effectiveness of the 1995 Reform Act and thus run contrary to SLUSA's stated purpose, viz., "to prevent certain State private securities class action lawsuits alleging fraud from being used to frustrate the objectives" of the 1995 Act. SLUSA §2(5), 112 Stat. 3227. As the *Blue Chip Stamps* Court observed, class actions brought by holders pose a special risk of vexatious litigation. *421 U.S., at 739 . . . .* It would be odd, to say the least, if SLUSA exempted that particularly troublesome subset of class actions from its pre-emptive sweep. *See Kircher, 403 F.3d at 484.*

Respondent's preferred construction also would give rise to wasteful, duplicative litigation. Facts supporting an action by purchasers under

Rule 10b-5 (which must proceed in federal court if at all) typically support an action by holders as well, at least in those States that recognize holder claims. The prospect is raised, then, of parallel class actions proceeding in state and federal court, with different standards governing claims asserted on identical facts. That prospect, which exists to some extent in this very case, squarely conflicts with the congressional preference for "national standards for securities class action lawsuits involving nationally traded securities." SLUSA §2(5), 112 Stat. 3227.[12]

In *Zandford*, we observed that the SEC has consistently "maintained that a broker who accepts payment for securities that he never intends to deliver, or who sells customer securities with intent to misappropriate the proceeds, violates *§10(b)* and *Rule 10b-5*." *535 U.S., at 819* . . . . Here, too, the SEC supports a broad reading of the "in connection with" language.

In concluding that SLUSA pre-empts state-law holder class-action claims of the kind alleged in Dabit's complaint, we do not lose sight of the general "presum[ption] that Congress does not cavalierly pre-empt state-law causes of action." *Medtronic, Inc. v. Lohr, 518 U.S. 470 . . . (1996).* But that presumption carries less force here than in other contexts because SLUSA does not actually pre-empt any state cause of action. It simply denies plaintiffs the right to use the class action device to vindicate certain claims. The Act does not deny any individual plaintiff, or indeed any group of fewer than 50 plaintiffs, the right to enforce any state-law cause of action that may exist.

Moreover, the tailored exceptions to SLUSA's pre-emptive command demonstrate that Congress did not by any means act "cavalierly" here. The statute carefully exempts from its operation certain class actions based on the law of the State in which the issuer of the covered security is incorporated, actions brought by a state agency or state pension plan, actions under contracts between issuers and indenture trustees, and derivative actions brought by shareholders on behalf of a corporation. . . . The statute also expressly preserves state jurisdiction over state agency enforcement proceedings. . . . The existence of these carve-outs both evinces congressional sensitivity to state prerogatives in this field and makes it inappropriate for courts to create additional, implied exceptions.

Finally, federal law, not state law, has long been the principal vehicle for asserting class-action securities fraud claims. *See, e.g.,* H. R. Conf. Rep. No. 105-803, p 14 (1998) ("Prior to the passage of the Reform Act, there was essentially no significant securities class action litigation brought in

---

12. *See* H. R. Rep. No. 105-640, p 10 (1998) (the "solution" to circumvention of the Reform Act "is to make Federal court the exclusive venue for securities fraud class action litigation"); S. Rep. No. 105-182, p 3 (1998) (identifying "the danger of maintaining differing federal and state standards of liability for nationally-traded securities").

State court"). More importantly, while state-law holder claims were theoretically available both before and after the decision in *Blue Chip Stamps*, the actual assertion of such claims by way of class action was virtually unheard of before SLUSA was enacted; respondent and his *amici* have identified only *one* pre-SLUSA case involving a state-law class action asserting holder claims. This is hardly a situation, then, in which a federal statute has eliminated a historically entrenched state-law remedy. . . .

V.

The holder class action that respondent tried to plead, and that the Second Circuit envisioned, is distinguishable from a typical *Rule 10b-5* class action in only one respect: It is brought by holders instead of purchasers or sellers. For purposes of SLUSA pre-emption, that distinction is irrelevant; the identity of the plaintiffs does not determine whether the complaint alleges fraud "in connection with the purchase or sale" of securities. The misconduct of which respondent complains here—fraudulent manipulation of stock prices—unquestionably qualifies as fraud "in connection with the purchase or sale" of securities as the phrase is defined in *Zandford, 535 U.S., at 820, 822 . . .* , and *O'Hagan, 521 U.S., at 651 . . . .*

The judgment of the Court of Appeals for the Second Circuit is vacated, and the case is remanded for further proceedings consistent with this opinion.

It is so ordered.

2. Who's Liable for Securities Fraud: Primary and Secondary Liability

b. Primary Participants

Page 767.   Before the Notes and Questions insert the following.

Simpson v. AOL Time Warner Inc.
452 F.3d 1040 (9th Cir. 2006)

GOULD, Circuit Judge:

This consolidated class action litigation alleges that multiple actors engaged in a scheme to commit securities fraud by overstating the reported revenues of an Internet company, Homestore.com

("Homestore"). Homestore eventually restated its revenues, resulting in a decrease in revenues of more than $170 million and corresponding declines in Homestore's stock value. The district court dismissed the securities claims against Defendants-Appellees, relying on the Supreme Court's decision in *Central Bank of Denver, N.A. v. First Interstate Bank of Denver, N.A., 511 U.S. 164 . . . (1994). . . .*

The Supreme Court held in *Central Bank* that *§10(b)* does not allow recovery for aiding and abetting liability, . . . but cautioned that secondary actors were not always free from liability under *§10(b)* because they may still be liable as a primary violator. . . . We address here the scope of primary violation liability that the Supreme Court did not fully define in *Central Bank. . . .*

I

CalSTRS [California State Teachers' Retirement System] alleges in its First Amended Consolidated Complaint ("FACC") that Homestore and its officers, along with its auditor PriceWaterhouseCoopers ("PWC"), AOL . . . additional Third Party Vendors, committed securities fraud by engaging in round-trip or barter transactions whereby Homestore recorded net revenues from its receipt of monies that came from Homestore's own cash reserves.

Homestore created an online real estate website in 1996. In the late 1990s, there was an explosion of Internet start-up companies which consistently posted net losses and negative cash flows as those companies sought to develop leadership and market share in their industries. This development caused a corresponding shift in emphasis by financial analysts to the tracking and evaluation of revenues as an indicator of future earnings. Until 2001, Homestore was perceived as an Internet company that consistently matched or exceeded its estimated revenue goals. To meet its revenue expectations, Homestore relied increasingly on barter or round-trip transactions with other companies. In such transactions, Homestore paid a company, the company returned part of the money to Homestore by way of a different transaction, and Homestore recorded these returned funds as revenue.

Internet companies have historically engaged in barter transactions between themselves, often in order to place advertising on each other's websites. Beginning in fiscal year 2000, the SEC implemented a new accounting standard that required companies engaging in barter transactions to report only the net revenue that was earned from these related transactions, rather than the gross revenue received. Facing increasing scrutiny from its auditor PWC, Homestore's barter transactions grew more complex. Homestore engaged in triangular transactions, with the result that PWC did not recognize that the revenue that Homestore recorded was related to a prior transaction funded by Homestore. As the district court succinctly summarized, in these triangular transactions:

> Homestore would find some third party corporation, one that was thinly capitalized and in search of revenues in order to "go public." Homestore then agreed to purchase shares in that company for inflated values or to purchase services or products that Homestore did not need. This transaction was contingent on the third party company "agreeing" to buy advertising from AOL for most or all of what Homestore was paying them. The money thus flowed through the third party to AOL, which then took a commission and shared "revenue" with Homestore.

In re Homestore.com, Inc. Securities Litigation, 252 F. Supp. 2d 1018, 1023 (C.D. Cal. 2003). Against this background, we consider the allegations against the particular Defendants.

A.   ALLEGATIONS INVOLVING AOL, AND ITS OFFICERS KELLER AND COLBURN

The history of Homestore and AOL for purposes of this appeal began with the creation of a legitimate partnership in April 1998, whereby Homestore purchased the "exclusive right to have the only online real estate listing product on AOL." In a second legitimate deal with AOL, Homestore entered into an advertising reseller agreement, under which AOL agreed in March 1999 to sell advertising on the Homestore website and retain a commission.

The triangular transactions at issue here occurred during the first two quarters of fiscal year 2001. Plaintiff alleges that Homestore entered into a series of sham transactions with various Third Party Vendors for some product or service that Homestore did not need. The Third Party Vendors would then contract with AOL for advertising on Homestore's website and AOL would give this money back to Homestore under their advertising reseller agreement. Both the Third Party Vendors and AOL would keep a portion of the money as a commission. Plaintiff only alleges that the first leg of the transaction was truly a sham because nothing of value was given in exchange for Homestore's payment. AOL continued to sell advertising on Homestore's website to Third Party Vendors, withholding commissions before passing the Vendors' payments on to Homestore.

Plaintiff alleges that Defendant Eric Keller, as an employee of AOL, jointly developed these transactions with Homestore. Keller was also alleged to have contacted some of the Third Party Vendors that took part in these triangular transactions. Plaintiff alleges, without detailed support, that Defendant Colburn, Keller's supervisor, approved the improper transactions. AOL placed Keller on administrative leave in June 2001. AOL then attempted to include more accurate documentation of the round trip nature of additional triangular transactions that occurred at the close of the second quarter of 2001. Homestore convinced AOL to accept less descriptive documents, which would not alert PWC to the nature of the round-trip transaction. AOL included a list of the "potential referral advertisers" as part of the second deal in 2001, but let Homestore add other companies not involved in the round-trip transactions so that the Third Party Vendors could not be identified. . . .

III . . .

A. THE USE OR EMPLOYMENT OF A DECEPTIVE DEVICE OR CONTRIVANCE

The Supreme Court tells us that *§10(b)* is intended to prohibit the use or employment of any deceptive device in connection with the purchase or sale of securities, including deception as part of a larger scheme to defraud the securities market. *See Ernst & Ernst, 425 U.S. at 199 n.20* (defining "device" as "an invention; project; scheme; often, a scheme to deceive"). . . . The Supreme Court has also held that a non-speaking actor who engages in a "scheme to defraud" has used or employed a deceptive device within the meaning of *§10(b)*. *See SEC v. Zandford, 535 U.S. 813, 821-221 . . . (2002).*

In *Central Bank*, the Supreme Court held that liability under *§10(b)* only extends to "primary violators" and there is no liability for merely "aiding and abetting" a violation. *511 U.S. at 191.* Since *Central Bank*, it is the duty of courts to determine what constitutes a "primary violation" of *§10(b)*. With respect to the making of false statements or omissions, we have held that "substantial participation or intricate involvement in the preparation of fraudulent statements is grounds for primary liability even though that participation might not lead to the actor's actual making of the statements." *Howard v. Everex Sys., Inc., 228 F.3d 1057, 1061 n.5 (9th Cir. 2000); see id. at 1061* (holding that signing and attesting to a statement, such that for all intents and purposes the signor-attestor made the statement, is sufficient to be considered a primary violator); *see also In re Software Toolworks Inc. Sec. Litig., 50 F.3d 615, 628-29 & n. 3 (9th Cir. 1994)* (holding that drafting or editing false statements that the drafter-editor knows will be publicly disseminated is sufficient to be considered a primary violator).

What it means to be a "primary violator" with respect to an alleged "scheme to defraud" has been less extensively discussed. In *Cooper v. Pickett, 137 F.3d 616, 624 (9th Cir. 1997)*, we held that to be liable for a "scheme to defraud," "each defendant [must have] committed a manipulative or deceptive act in furtherance of the scheme." The relevant inquiry is: what conduct constitutes a manipulative or deceptive act in the furtherance of a scheme to defraud sufficient to render the defendant a "primary violator" of *§10(b)*?

The SEC argues in its amicus brief that "Any person who directly or indirectly engages in a manipulative or deceptive act as part of a scheme to defraud can be a primary violator." The SEC defines "a deceptive act" as "engaging in a transaction whose principal purpose and effect is to create a false appearance of revenues." We agree with the SEC that engaging in a transaction, the principal purpose and effect of which is to create the false appearance of fact, constitutes a "deceptive act." Participation in a fraudulent transaction by itself, however, is insufficient to qualify the defendant as a "primary violator" if the deceptive nature of the transaction or scheme was not an intended result, at least in part, of the defendant's own conduct. We hold that to be liable as a primary violator of *§10(b)* for participation in a "scheme to defraud," the defendant must have engaged in conduct that had the principal purpose and effect of creating a false appearance of fact in furtherance of the scheme. It is not enough that a *transaction* in which a defendant was involved had a deceptive purpose and effect; the defendant's *own conduct* contributing to the transaction or overall scheme must have had a deceptive purpose and effect.[2]

---

2. The "principal purpose" prong is related to but different from the element of scienter. . . . While the scienter element ensures a culpable state of mind and must be satisfied for recovery under *§10(b)*, the "principal purpose" prong examines instead whether the challenged conduct of the defendant had a principal purpose, and not just an accidental effect, of creating a false appearance as part of a deceptive transaction or fraudulent scheme. Unlike the scienter requirement, the "purpose and effect" test is focused on differentiating conduct that may form the basis of a primary violation under *§10(b)* from mere aiding and abetting activity that the Supreme Court has held does not constitute a primary violation. A defendant may intend to deceive the public by substantially assisting another's misconduct as part of a scheme to defraud, but fail to perform personally any action that created a false appearance as part of this scheme. The scienter requirement, therefore, will not in all cases distinguish aiding and abetting from primary liability. In applying the "scienter" element, we look at whether a defendant's state of mind was sufficiently culpable for *§10(b)* liability. By contrast, we may examine the "principal purpose and effect" of the defendant's challenged conduct in a fraudulent scheme as an aid to assessing whether the defendant's conduct was sufficiently deceptive for *§10(b)* liability.

Defendants argue that imposing liability for participation in an overall scheme to defraud would impose liability for conduct other than the making of a material misstatement or omission and would conflict with *Central Bank*. We disagree. We see no justification to limit liability under §10(b) to only those who draft or edit the statements released to the public. To the contrary, §10(b) prohibits any person or entity from using or employing any deceptive device, directly or indirectly, in connection with the purchase and sale of securities. *See* Robert A. Prentice, *Locating That "Indistinct" and "Virtually Nonexistent" Line Between Primary and Secondary Liability under Section 10(b)*, 75 N.C. L. Rev. 691, 731 (1997) (asserting that "the view that one can be liable only for one's own statements arguably ignores the fact that both *Section 10(b)* and *Rule 10b-5* condemn those who employ devices or make misstatements 'directly or indirectly'"). Furthermore, §10(b) "should be construed not technically and restrictively, but flexibly to effectuate its remedial purposes." *Zandford*, 535 U.S. at 819 (internal quotation marks omitted). Nor is "scheme to defraud" liability a substitute for aiding and abetting liability that the Supreme Court precludes in *Central Bank*. The focus of the inquiry on the deceptive nature of the defendant's own conduct ensures that only primary violators (that is, only those defendants who use or employ a manipulative or deceptive device) are held liable under the Act. . . .

Conduct by the defendant that does not have a principal legitimate business purpose, such as the invention of sham corporate entities to misrepresent the flow of income, may have a principal purpose of creating a false appearance. *See In re Enron Corp. Sec., Derivative & "ERISA" Litig.*, 310 F. Supp. 2d 819, 830 (S.D. Tex. 2004) ("Sham business transactions with no legitimate business purpose that are actually guaranteed 'loans' employed to inflate Enron['s] financial image are not above-board business practices."). Conduct that is consistent with the defendants' normal course of business would not typically be considered to have the purpose and effect of creating a misrepresentation. *See In re Enron Corp. Sec., Derivative & ERISA Litig.*, 235 F. Supp. 2d 549, 580 (S.D. Tex. 2002) (finding that "conclusory allegations that are consistent with the normal activity of such a business entity, standing alone, . . . are insufficient to state a claim of primary liability under *Central Bank*" (internal quotation marks omitted)). Participation in a legitimate transaction, which does not have a deceptive purpose or effect, would not allow for a primary violation even if the defendant knew or intended that another party would manipulate the transaction to effectuate a fraud. . . . *In re Parmalat Sec. Litig.*, 376 F. Supp. 2d 472, 505 (S.D.N.Y. 2005) ("At worst, the banks designed and entered into the transactions knowing or even intending that Parmalat or its auditors would misrepresent the nature of the arrangements. That is, they substantially assisted fraud with culpable knowledge — in other words, they aided and abetted it.").

If a defendant's conduct or role in an illegitimate transaction has the principal purpose and effect of creating a false appearance of fact in the furtherance of a scheme to defraud, then the defendant is using or employing a deceptive device within the meaning of *§10(b)*. A test that examines the purpose and effect of a defendant's conduct in an alleged scheme to defraud, as a means to assess whether the defendant used or employed a deceptive device, ensures that the defendant's conduct is sufficiently deceptive to justify imposing primary liability. Thus, when determining whether a defendant is a "primary violator," the conduct of each defendant, while evaluated in its context, must be viewed alone for whether it had the purpose and effect of creating a false appearance of fact in the furtherance of an overall scheme to defraud.

B.   IN CONNECTION WITH THE PURCHASE OR SALE OF SECURITIES

In addition to the use or employment of a deceptive or manipulative device or contrivance, *§10(b)* requires that the primary violation must be "in connection with the purchase or sale of any security." . . .

[A] scheme to misrepresent the publicly reported revenue of a company may coincide with the purchase or sale of securities because the scheme will not be complete until the fraudulent information is introduced into the securities market. That every participant in the scheme did not release the information to the public does not diminish the causal connection between all defendants in the scheme and the securities market. . . . If multiple participants used or employed a deceptive device in furtherance of a scheme to misrepresent the reported revenues of a company, then all participants may be viewed as having acted in connection with the purchase or sale of securities.

C.   RELIANCE

Another requirement for liability under *§10(b)* is reliance. *See Cent. Bank, 511 U.S. at 180*. "Reliance provides the requisite causal connection between a defendant's misrepresentation and a plaintiff's injury." *Basic Inc. v. Levinson, 485 U.S. 224, 243, 108 S. Ct. 978, 99 L. Ed. 2d 194 (1988)*. A plaintiff may be presumed to have relied on a misrepresentation if the misleading or false information was injected into an efficient market. . . . The fraud-on-the-market presumption requires the dissemination of the misrepresentation into an efficient market, but not personal involvement by the defendant in disseminating this statement. *See Knapp v. Ernst & Whinney, 90 F.3d 1431, 1436 (9th Cir. 1996).* . . .

The requirement of reliance is satisfied if the introduction of misleading statements into the securities market was the intended end result of a scheme to misrepresent revenue. *See In re ZZZZ Best Sec. Litig., 864 F. Supp. 960, 973 (C.D. Cal. 1994).* . . . We may presume, absent persuasive conflicting evidence, that purchasers relied on misstatements produced by a defendant as part of a scheme to defraud, even if the defendant did not publish or release the misrepresentations directly to the securities market.

We conclude that conduct by a defendant that had the principal purpose and effect of creating a false appearance in deceptive transactions as part of a scheme to defraud is conduct that uses or employs a deceptive device within the meaning of *§10(b)*. Furthermore, such conduct may be in connection with the purchase or sale of securities if it is part of a scheme to misrepresent public financial information where the scheme is not complete until the misleading information is disseminated into the securities market. Finally, a plaintiff may be presumed to have relied on this scheme to defraud if a misrepresentation, which necessarily resulted from the scheme and the defendant's conduct therein, was disseminated into an efficient market and was reflected in the market price.

IV

With these principles in mind, we address the adequacy of the allegations of the FACC at issue here. . . .

A. PRIMARY LIABILITY OF AMERICA ONLINE (AOL) AND ITS OFFICERS

AOL and its officers are alleged to have played a role in the scheme to overstate the revenues of Homestore. According to the FACC, Eric Keller, a Senior Vice President at AOL, helped Homestore to organize and create the triangular transactions. The FACC further alleges that the triangular transactions were necessary to allow Homestore to overstate its revenues, and that the actions of AOL, Colburn and Keller assisted Homestore in misrepresenting the revenues from these transactions. . . .

It is not alleged that AOL or its officers created sham business entities or engaged in deceptive conduct as part of illegitimate transactions, and so we conclude that the element of using or employing a deceptive device is not adequately alleged in this respect. There is no indication from the FACC that the transactions engaged in by AOL were completely illegitimate or in themselves created a false appearance.[3] The substance of the allegations shows that AOL's role in the transactions was to act as a conduit for the flow of revenue between the Third Party Vendors and Homestore as an advertising agent, in accord with AOL's advertising reseller agreement with Homestore.

The FACC does allege that Homestore entered into sham transactions with "Third Party Vendors" in return for a "quid pro quo" obligation from these vendors to buy Homestore advertising from AOL. Assuming the truth of allegations that no products of value were exchanged between the Third Party Vendors and Homestore, the FACC nonetheless does not allege that AOL itself entered into a transaction that had no legitimate economic value or created a false appearance. While the advertising transactions between the Third Party Vendors and AOL are alleged to contain suspect qualities, such as exaggerated commissions by AOL, there is no suggestion that actual advertisements were not purchased and sold by these companies. The FACC does not allege that the transactions contained a false appearance or other deceptive qualities, but rather that they were an opportunity for Homestore to take advantage of the advertising reseller agreement. This may pin liability on Homestore, but not on AOL or its officers.

The FACC also alleges that AOL attempted to include additional documentation in subsequent transactions that would connect the referral agreements between Homestore and the Third Party Vendors with the advertising revenues from AOL. While the absence of this additional documentation allowed Homestore to misreport the revenues from the AOL advertising referrals as stand-alone transactions, any misrepresentation in the transactions involving AOL resulted from the additional agreements between Homestore and the Third Party Vendors and the misreporting of the income by Homestore. The transactions involving AOL did not create a false appearance until they were viewed in conjunction with Homestore's actions before and after the transaction. While AOL would be liable under §10(b) for its deceptive conduct as part of a scheme to defraud if AOL engaged in deceptive conduct, it may not be held liable for participating in legitimate transactions that became "deceptive" only when distorted by the willful or intentional fraud of another party. See Parmalat, 376 F. Supp. 2d at 505 ("Any deceptiveness resulted from the manner in which Parmalat or its auditors described the transactions on Parmalat's balance sheets and elsewhere."). In this case, the FACC does not allege with the required particularity that the

---

3. Defendants urge that the challenged transactions were not deceptive, and that only the reporting of revenues from these transactions by Homestore, conduct in which Homestore was not assisted by the Defendants, deceived the investing public about revenues of Homestore.

transactions negotiated by Keller and performed by AOL created a false appearance.

We conclude that the FACC failed to sufficiently allege with particularity that AOL committed actions with the purpose and effect of creating a false appearance in furtherance of a scheme to defraud.

VI

We affirm the district court's dismissal of the current complaint against Defendants. We remand so that Plaintiff may seek leave in the district court to amend the complaint if that can be done consistent with this opinion. Costs are awarded to Defendants-Appellees.

AFFIRMED and REMANDED for further proceedings consistent with this opinion.

Page 767.   Add the following to note 1.

Recently, the Second Circuit held that the failure of an accountant to correct or update its earlier certified opinion of its client's financial statements can subject the accountant to primary liability. *See Overton v. Todman & Co., CPAs, P.C.,* 2007 U.S. App. LEXIS 4239 (2d Cir. 2007). From 1999 to 2002, the CPA had certified its client's financial statements. The plaintiff alleged the auditior failed to correct or withdraw the earlier certifications, ignoring various warning signs that the financial statements were misleading. The Second Circuit held that primary liability under Rule 10b-5 arises when the auditor subsequently learns or is reckless in not learning that the earlier statements were misleading and fails to take reasonable steps to correct or withdraw its opinion.

3.   Rescission and Restitution of Contracts in Violation of the Securities Laws

Page 789.   Add the following before Problem 13-8.

4. Where's the Violation? Where's the Transaction? Helpful guidance on the scope of Section 29(b) is provided by *GFL Advantage Fund, Ltd. v. Colkitt,* 272 F.3d 189 (3d Cir. 2001). GFL advanced $13 million to Colkitt in exchange for his promise at some future date to repay GFL by transferring shares in a publicly traded company. The number of shares was to be determined by their then market price, less a discount of 17 percent. Colkitt alleged that GFL, through a series of short sales, had artificially depressed the company shares for the purpose of increasing the number of shares that Colkitt would have to deliver to satisfy the loan. He therefore sought to rescind the arrangement under Section 29(b). The Third Circuit dismissed the suit, reasoning that for relief under Section 29(b) the securities violation must be inseparable from the underlying agreement. Such a relationship exists when the agreement cannot be carried out without violating the securities laws. The court viewed the alleged short sales as "down stream" transactions that were independent of the lending agreement Colkitt sought to rescind.

Mr. Colkitt's quest for funds spawned another interesting application of Section 29(b) in *Berckeley Investment Group, Ltd. v. Colkitt*, 455 F.3d 195 (3d Cir. 2006). Colkitt alleged that Berckeley recklessly misrepresented that it would not violate the securities laws with respect to securities to be delivered by Colkitt in satisfaction of a loan Berckeley had made to Colkitt. Since Colkitt was not the purchaser of shares allegedly sold in violation of Section 5 of the Securities Act, the remedy provided in Section 12(a)(1) was not available to him. And, by proceeding under Section 29(b) instead of the antifraud provision, Section 10(b) and Rule 10b-5, Colkitt sought to avoid a ticklish reliance issue. Albeit, the provision of the securities law upon which he premised his Section 29(b) action was the antifraud provision. Learning from his earlier want of success, he alleged misrepresentations in the lending agreement itself and the surrounding negotiations. The court reversed the district court's grant of Berckeley's motion of summary judgment on the grounds there were triable issues of fact related to whether Berckeley had engaged in a reckless misrepresentation. Would you lend money to this man?

B.   Enforcement Actions by the SEC

1.   Investigations

b.   Recommendations to the Commission

Page 807.   Add the following after the Note and Questions heading.

1.   When Is It Appropriate to Fine the Entity?   The Commission recently adopted a statement setting forth considerations it would use in determining whether to impose financial penalties on an entity whose agents had engaged in a securities violation in the scope of performing their employment. *See* Statement of the SEC Concerning Financial Penalties, Press Rel. 2006-4 (Jan. 4, 2006). The Commission sought an approach that would grapple with two competing fears: that sanctions imposed on the entity may adversely impact its innocent shareholder-owners and that failure to sanction the entity may erode the deterrent effect of the enforcement action or permit ill-gotten gains to be retained.

It identified two principal considerations in sanctioning a corporation:

1. The presence or absence of a direct benefit to the corporation as a result of the violation; and
2. The degree to which the penalty will recompense or further harm the injured shareholders.

In addition to these two principal considerations, the Commission stated the following additional factors are in appropriate cases to be considered:

1. The need to deter the particular offense;
2. The extent of the injury to innocent parties;
3. Whether complicity in the violation is widespread throughout the corporation;
4. The level of intent on the part of the perpetrators;
5. The degree of difficulty in detecting the type of offense;
6. The presence or lack of remedial steps by the corporation; and
7. The extent of cooperation with the Commission and other law enforcement agencies.

PROBLEM 13-11A.

After a lengthy SEC investigation, Brobade Inc. recently proposed a settlement with the SEC agreeing to restate its reported earnings for the past five years. The restatement reflects widespread backdating of stock options by a committee of executives who repeatedly approved option grant dates that were much earlier than the dates options were in fact awarded. The dates selected yield prices that were materially lower than the price of its shares on the actual grant date. The effect of this difference was that upon the grant of an option the recipient experienced an immediate financial benefit because the option when granted was "in the money."

Anticipating shareholder litigation and hoping to preserve the attorney-client privilege for the nondisclosed portions of the report, Brobade refused to share with the SEC the results of an internal investigation that had been carried out by an outside law firm that had no historical relationship with the company. The company did disclose to the SEC excerpts from the report showing that about 75 percent of the backdated options went to senior management. Brobade explained that the backdating practices were widespread in the industry and that it engaged in the practice so as to recruit and retain high-quality personnel. A schedule from the report that was released to the SEC showed that about 60 percent of the individuals who received backdated options were employees who had before the grant been with the company less than three months.

The SEC enforcement staff recommends that no settlement be approved unless Brobade agrees to pay a substantial financial penalty. The matter is now before the Commissioners. On these facts, is a penalty appropriate under the SEC's 2006 guidelines? What additional facts would you wish to know in making this decision?

E.   Enforcement of the Securities Laws in the Criminal Justice System

1.   The Criminal Provisions of the Federal Securities Laws

Page 868.   Add the following at the end of note 2.

3.   GAAP in the Criminal Case.   As seen earlier in Chapter 10, *United States v. Simon*, 425 F.2d 796 (2d Cir. 1969), held that compliance with generally accepted auditing and accounting standards is not an ironclad defense in a criminal case. This principle was recently invoked in the criminal case arising from the collapse of WorldCom, whose CEO, Bernard Ebbers, ultimately received a 25-year sentence for his role in the largest accounting fraud to date. *United States v. Ebbers*, 458 F.3d 110 (2d Cir. 2006). Ebbers repeatedly instructed his CFO and other accounting personnel that WorldCom "had to make its numbers," referring to meeting analysts' expectations regarding the company's revenue and earnings growth. To achieve these results, the court found that Ebbers and his staff creatively employed accounting steps to inflate revenues and conceal costs. For example, to boost revenues for a quarter, they included in revenues estimated "underutilization penalties" for certain customers, even though they did not expect these sums would be collectible. The bulk of the financial manipulation was their systematic recording of billions of dollars of operating costs as assets rather than expenses. In appealing his conviction, Ebbers argued that the government should have been required to prove that these actions violated GAAP. Invoking *Simon*, the court disagreed:

> In a real sense, by alleging and proving that the financial statements were misleading, the government did, in fact, allege and prove violations of GAAP. According to the AICPA's Codification of Statements in Accounting Standards, AU §312.04, "financial statements are materially misstated when they contain misstatements whose effect, individually or in the aggregate, is important enough to cause them not to be fairly, in all material respects, in compliance with GAAP." Thus, GAAP itself recognizes that technical compliance with particular GAAP rules may lead to misleading financial statements, and imposes an overall requirement that the statements as a whole accurately reflect the financial status of the company.
>
> To be sure . . . differences of opinion as to GAAP's requirements may be relevant to the defendant's intent where financial statements are prepared in a good faith attempt to comply with GAAP. The rules are no shield, however, in a case such as the present one, where evidence showed that the accounting methods known to be misleading — although perhaps at times fortuitously in compliance with GAAP rules — were used for the express purpose of intentionally misstating WorldCom's financial condition and artificially inflating its stock price.

Id. at 126.

2. Mail and Wire Fraud

Page 873.   At the end of the text before the heading, add the following.

But how about executives who materially misrepresent the financial position and performance of their employer so as the advance the firm's interest? Have the executives deprived their employer of "honest services"? In *United States v. Brown*, 459 F.3d 509 (5th Cir. 2006), Enron, the employer, created an incentive structure that encouraged achievement of earnings goals, which in turn provided the incentive for the defendants to falsely report earnings. The court reasoned, "[W]here an employer intentionally aligns the interests of the employee with a specified corporate goal, where the employee perceives his pursuit of that goal as mutually benefiting him and his employer, and where the employee's conduct is consistent with that perception of the mutual interest, such conduct is beyond the reach of the honest-services theory of fraud. . . . " Id. at 522.

||14||
The Regulation of Insider Trading

D.   The Misappropriation Theory

Page 898.   Add the following at the end of note 3.

This was the situation that arose in a particularly interesting case, *SEC v. Rocklage*, 470 F.3d 1 (1st Cir. 2006): The wife of a company insider learned bad news about the company from her husband. She then conveyed this information "with a wink and a nod" to her brother, who sold stock he owned in the company — but only after the wife told her husband that she was about to do so. He strongly urged her not to, but she did anyway. The court acknowledged that, under the dicta in *O'Hagan*, these facts alone might pose a problem for imposing liability under the misappropriation theory. But it held that because the wife had a *preexisting* understanding with her brother that she would tip him if she learned negative information from her husband, the deceptive scheme arose well before her receipt of the information and her brother's trading. In other words, according to the court, her deception in concealing this scheme enabled her to obtain the information in the first place, and that was sufficient to constitute fraud in connection with the purchase or sale of the securities.

H. Insider Trading and Section 16

1. The Scope of Section 16(b)

Page 924.   Add the following at the end of the *Feder* case.

On remand, the district court granted defendant's motion for summary judgment, finding no material factual dispute that the Frost group was not a controlling shareholder of NAVI, and neither had nor shared investment control over NAVI's portfolio. Feder v. Frost, 98 Civ. 4744 (RO) (S.D.N.Y., Feb. 15, 2007).

15

Shareholder Voting and Going Private Transactions

A. The Election of Directors and Other Routine Matters

2. Shareholder Proposals

Page 939. At the beginning of subsection 2, insert the following.

American Federation of State, County & Municipal Employees v. American International Group, Inc.
462 F.3d 121 (2d Cir. 2006)

WESLEY, Circuit Judge:

The American Federation of State, County & Municipal Employees ("AFSCME") is one of the country's largest public service employee unions. Through its pension plan, AFSCME holds 26,965 shares of voting common stock of American International Group ("AIG" or "Company"), a multi-national corporation operating in the insurance and financial services sectors. On December 1, 2004, AFSCME submitted to AIG for inclusion in the Company's 2005 proxy statement a shareholder proposal that, if adopted by a majority of AIG shareholders at the Company's 2005 annual meeting, would amend the AIG bylaws to require the Company, under certain circumstances, to publish the names of shareholder-nominated candidates for director positions together with any candidates nominated by AIG's board of directors ("Proposal").[3] AIG sought the input of the Division regarding whether AIG could exclude the Proposal from its proxy statement under the election exclusion on the basis that it "relates to an election." The Division issued a no-action letter in which it indicated that it would not recommend an enforcement action against AIG should the Company exclude the Proposal from its proxy statement. . . .

DISCUSSION

Rule 14a-8(i)(8), also known as "the town meeting rule," regulates what are referred to as "shareholders proposals," that is, "recommendation[s] or requirement[s] that the company and/or its board of directors take [some] action, which [the submitting shareholder(s)] intend to present at a meeting of the company's shareholders." If a shareholder seeking to submit a proposal meets certain eligibility and procedural

---

3.   The AFSCME Proposal states in relevant part:

RESOLVED, pursuant to Section 6.9 of the By-laws (the "Bylaws") of American International Group Inc. ("AIG") and section 109(a) of the Delaware General Corporation Law, stockholders hereby amend the Bylaws to add section 6.10:
   "The Corporation shall include in its proxy materials for a meeting of stockholders the name, together with the Disclosure and Statement (both defined below), of any person nominated for election to the Board of Directors by a stockholder or group thereof that satisfies the requirements of this section 6.10 (the "Nominator"), and allow stockholders to vote with respect to such nominee on the Corporation's proxy card. Each Nominator may nominate one candidate for election at a meeting.
   To be eligible to make a nomination, a Nominator must:

(a)   have beneficially owned 3% or more of the Corporation's outstanding common stock (the "Required Shares") for at least one year;
(b)   provide written notice received by the Corporation's Secretary within the time period specified in section 1.11 of the Bylaws containing (i) with respect to the nominee, (A) the information required by Items 7(a), (b) and (c) of SEC Schedule 14A (such information is referred to herein as the "Disclosure") and (B) such nominee's consent to being named in the proxy statement and to serving as a director if elected; and (ii) with respect to the Nominator, proof of ownership of the Required Shares; and
(c)   execute an undertaking that it agrees (i) to assume all liability of any violation of law or regulation arising out of the Nominator's communications with stockholders, including the Disclosure (ii) to the extent it uses soliciting material other than the Corporation's proxy materials, comply with all laws and regulations relating thereto.

   The Nominator shall have the option to furnish a statement, not to exceed 500 words, in support of the nominee's candidacy (the "Statement"), at the time the Disclosure is submitted to the Corporation's Secretary. The Board of Directors shall adopt a procedure for timely resolving disputes over whether notice of a nomination was timely given and whether the Disclosure and Statement comply with this section 6.10 and SEC Rules."

requirements, the corporation is required to include the proposal in its proxy statement and identify the proposal in its form of proxy, unless the corporation can prove to the SEC that a given proposal may be excluded based on one of thirteen grounds enumerated in the regulations. One of these grounds, Rule 14a-8(i)(8), provides that a corporation may exclude a shareholder proposal "[i]f the proposal relates to an election for membership on the company's board of directors or analogous governing body."

We must determine whether, under Rule 14a-8(i)(8), a shareholder proposal "relates to an election" if it seeks to amend the corporate bylaws to establish a procedure by which certain shareholders are entitled to include in the corporate proxy materials their nominees for the board of directors ("proxy access bylaw proposal"). "In interpreting an administrative regulation, as in interpreting a statute, we must begin by examining the language of the provision at issue." *Resnik v. Swartz*, 303 F.3d 147, 151-52 (2d Cir. 2002) (citing *New York Currency Research Corp. v. CFTC*, 180 F.3d 83, 92 (2d Cir. 1999)). The relevant language here — "relates to an election" — is not particularly helpful. AFSCME reads the election exclusion as creating an obvious distinction between proposals addressing a particular seat in a particular election (which AFSCME concedes are excludable) and those, like AFSCME's proposal, that simply set the background rules governing elections generally (which AFSCME claims are not excludable). AFSCME's distinction rests on Rule 14a-8(i)(8)'s use of the article "an," which AFSCME claims "necessarily implies that the phrase 'relates to an election' is intended to relate to proposals that address *particular elections,* instead of simply 'elections' generally." It is at least plausible that the words "an election" were intended to narrow the scope of the election exclusion, confining its application to proposals relating to "a particular election *and not* elections generally." It is, however, also plausible that the phrase was intended to create a comparatively broader exclusion, one covering "a particular election *or* elections generally" since any proposal that relates to elections in general will necessarily relate to an election in particular. The language of Rule 14a8(i)(8) provides no reason to adopt one interpretation over the other.

When the language of a regulation is ambiguous, we typically look for guidance in any interpretation made by the agency that promulgated the regulation in question. We are aware of two statements published by the SEC that offer informal interpretations of Rule 14a-8(i)(8). The first is a statement appearing in the amicus brief that the SEC filed in this case at our request. The second interpretation is contained in a statement the SEC published in 1976, the last time the SEC revised the election exclusion. Neither of these interpretations has the force of law. But, while agency interpretations that lack the force of law do not warrant deference when they interpret ambiguous *statutes,* they do normally warrant deference when they interpret ambiguous *regulations.*

In its amicus brief, the SEC interprets Rule 14a-8(i)(8) as permitting the exclusion of shareholder proposals that "would result in contested elections." The SEC explains that "[f]or purposes of Rule 14a-8, a proposal would result in a contested election if it is a means either to campaign for or against a director nominee or to require a company to include shareholder-nominated candidates in the company's proxy materials." Under this interpretation, a proxy access bylaw proposal like AFSCME's would be excludable under Rule 14a-8(i)(8) because it "is a means to require AIG to include shareholder-nominated candidates in the company's proxy materials." However, that interpretation is plainly at odds with the interpretation the SEC made in 1976. . . .

Because the interpretation of Rule 14a-8(i)(8) that the SEC advances in its amicus brief—that the election exclusion applies to proxy access bylaw proposals—conflicts with the 1976 Statement, it does not merit the usual deference we would reserve for an agency's interpretation of its own regulations. . . . In its amicus submission, the SEC fails to so much as acknowledge a changed position, let alone offer a reasoned analysis of the change. The amicus brief is curiously silent on any Division action prior to 1990 and characterizes the intermittent post-1990 no-action letters which continued to apply the pre-1990 position as mere "mistake[s]." While we by no means wish to imply that the Commission or the Division cannot correct analytical errors following a refinement of their thinking, we have a difficult time accepting the SEC's characterization of a policy that the Division consistently applied for sixteen years as nothing more than a "mistake." Although we are willing to afford the Commission considerable latitude in explaining departures from prior interpretations, its reasoned analysis must consist of something more than *mea culpas.*

Accordingly, we deem it appropriate to defer to the 1976 Statement, which represents the SEC's interpretation of the election exclusion the last time the Rule was substantively revised.[8] We therefore interpret the

---

8. AIG suggests that the interpretation of the election exclusion that we adopt here—that it does not apply to proxy access proposals—"improperly conflicts" with a proposed SEC rule that would require corporations in particular circumstances to include certain shareholder-nominated director candidates in the corporate proxy statement. *See* Security Holder Director Nominations, SEC Exchange Act Release No. 34-48626, 68 Fed. Reg. 60,784, 60,787 (Oct. 14, 2003) ("Proposed Rule 14a-11"). Proposed Rule 14a-11 would entitle a holder of at least 5% of the corporation's voting stock to place a nominee on the corporate ballot but only if the proxy access rule had been "activated" by one of two triggering events, including the adoption, by majority vote, of a shareholder proposal submitted by a holder of more than 1% of the corporation's voting stock. Essentially, Proposed Rule 14a-11 establishes a process by which the shareholder proposal mechanism (subject to the heightened eligibility requirement that the proposal be submitted by a holder of more than 1% of the corporation's voting stock) may be employed to adopt a proxy access rule that is uniform across companies. We

election exclusion as applying to shareholder proposals that relate to a particular election and not to proposals that, like AFSCME's, would establish the procedural rules governing elections generally. In deeming proxy access bylaw proposals non-excludable under Rule 14a-8(i)(8), we take no side in the policy debate regarding shareholder access to the corporate ballot. There might be perfectly good reasons for permitting companies to exclude proposals like AFSCME's, just as there may well be valid policy reasons for rendering them non-excludable. However, Congress has determined that such issues are appropriately the province of the SEC, not the judiciary.

C.   "Solicitations"

Page 947. Add the following after note 4.

5.   Electronic Solicitations. The SEC has revised Reg. 14A to permit issuers and others soliciting shareholder proxies or consents to use a "notice and access" approach not unlike the new procedures for prospectus delivery under the '33 Act after the 2005 offering reforms, discussed in Chapter 4. *See Internet Availability of Proxy Materials*, Exch. Act Rel. 55146, Jan. 22, 2007. Those doing the soliciting can post all the relevant disclosures on a publicly available web site, and simply send a notice by mail (or e-mail if the shareholder has already consented to electronic delivery) of that availability. This is designed to save substantially on printing and mailing costs. A shareholder who wants a printed copy of the materials may request one.

Those making solicitations on behalf of persons other than the issuer can do the same, and, unlike issuers, they can choose to solicit fewer than all shareholders if they wish — they need not make information available to everyone. The SEC has indicated that this should make it considerably less expensive for institutional investors and others to campaign against incumbents or oppose a solicitation by management.

---

recognize that our holding facilitates a process, by means of shareholder proposals subject to the standard eligibility requirements, for adopting non-uniform proxy access rules that are less restrictive than that created by Proposed Rule 14a-11. Thus, there might very well be no reason for a rule based on Proposed Rule 14a-11 to co-exist with the procedure that our holding makes available to shareholders. Accordingly, if the Commission ultimately decides to adopt Proposed Rule 14a11, then such an action, although certainly not necessary, would likely be sufficient to modify the interpretation of Rule 14a-8(i)(8) that we have adopted here.

‖16‖
Corporate Takeovers

C. Tender Offer Regulation: Controlling the Bidder

3. Substantive Regulation

d. The "All Holders-Best Price" Rule

Page 989.   At the end of note 1, insert the following.

In Exchange Act Release 54684 (Nov. 1, 2006), the SEC revised Rule 14d-10 to make it clear that, with very limited exceptions, the rule does not apply to compensatory or severance arrangements with target company officers and directors. A safe harbor was created to offer even greater certainty for compensatory payments that have been approved by independent directors of the subject company or the bidder. The revised rule also sought to resolve the split in the circuits generated by cases such as *Epstein* and *Lerro* by indicating that only consideration paid to security holders for securities tendered into a tender offer will be evaluated when determining the highest consideration paid to other holders.

‖18‖

The Investment Advisers and Investment Company Acts of 1940

A. The Regulation of Investment Advisers

1. The Registration Requirement

Page 1082. **At the end of the second to the last paragraph, insert the following.**

In *Goldstein v. SEC*, 451 F.3d 873 (D.C. Cir. 2006), the court struck down the SEC's hedge fund rule, finding that the statutory exemption for advisers with fewer than 15 clients was clear enough on its face and in its legislative history that the Commission could not alter its meaning by counting each of the hedge fund's investors as a separate client.

B. Mutual Funds and Other Investment Companies

2. The Structure and Governance of Mutual Funds

Page 1104. **At the end of the carryover paragraph, add the following.**

In *Chamber of Commerce v. SEC*, 443 F.3d 890 (D.C. Cir. 2006), the D.C. Circuit again invalidated the rule, finding the hurried analysis of the rule's costs still deficient.

S-1 Registration Statement for Weight Watchers International, Inc.

SECURITIES AND EXCHANGE COMMISSION
WASHINGTON, D.C. 20549

FORM S-1

REGISTRATION STATEMENT
UNDER
THE SECURITIES ACT OF 1933

WEIGHT WATCHERS INTERNATIONAL, INC.

VIRGINIA   7299   11-6040273

175 CROSSWAYS PARK WEST
WOODBURY, NEW YORK 11797-2055
(516) 390-1400

ROBERT HOLLWEG, ESQ.
WEIGHT WATCHERS INTERNATIONAL, INC.
175 CROSSWAYS PARK WEST
WOODBURY, NEW YORK 11797-2055
(516) 390-1400
WITH COPIES TO:

RISE B. NORMAN, ESQ.   KRIS F. HEINZELMAN, ESQ.
SIMPSON THACHER & BARTLETT   CRAVATH, SWAINE & MOORE
425 LEXINGTON AVENUE   825 EIGHTH AVENUE
NEW YORK, NEW YORK 10017   NEW YORK, NEW YORK 10019

APPROXIMATE DATE OF COMMENCEMENT OF PROPOSED SALE TO THE PUBLIC: As soon as practicable after this registration statement becomes effective.

If any of the securities being registered on this Form are to be offered on a delayed or continuous basis pursuant to Rule 415 under the Securities Act of 1933, check the following box. ☐

If this Form is filed to register additional securities for an offering pursuant to Rule 462(b) under the Securities Act, please check the following box. ☐

If this Form is a post-effective amendment filed pursuant to Rule 462(c) under the Securities Act, check the following box and list the Securities Act registration statement number of the earlier effective registration statement for the same offering. ☐

If this Form is a post-effective amendment filed pursuant to Rule 462(d) under the Securities Act, check the following box and list the Securities Act registration statement number of the earlier effective registration statement for the same offering. ☐

If delivery of the prospectus is expected to be made pursuant to Rule 434, please check the following box. ☐

CALCULATION OF REGISTRATION FEE

TITLE OF EACH CLASS OF SECURITIES TO BE REGISTERED	AMOUNT TO BE REGISTERED[1]	PROPOSED MAXIMUM OFFERING PRICE PER UNIT	PROPOSED AGGREGATE OFFERING PRICE[2]	AMOUNT OF REGISTRATION FEE[3]
Common stock, no par value........	20,010,000 shares	$25.00	$500,250,000	$10,005
Preferred stock purchase rights[4] ...	—	—	—	—
Total.............................	20,010,000 shares	$25.00	$500,250,000	$10,005

[1] Includes 2,610,000 shares subject to the underwriters' over-allotment option.

[2] Estimated solely for the purpose of calculating the amount of the registration fee pursuant to Rule 457(o).

[3] $25,000 of the total registration fee of $125,063 was paid on September 13, 2001, prior to the initial filing of the registration statement. $90,058 of the total registration fee of $125,063 was paid on October 29, 2001, prior to the filing of Amendment No. 1 to the registration statement. Therefore, the total registration fee payable upon the filing of this Amendment No. 3, calculated in accordance with Rule 457(a), is $10,005.

[4] The preferred stock purchase rights initially will trade together with the common stock. The value attributable to the preferred stock purchase rights, if any, is reflected in the offering price of the common stock.

THE REGISTRANT HEREBY AMENDS THIS REGISTRATION STATEMENT ON SUCH DATE OR DATES AS MAY BE NECESSARY TO DELAY ITS EFFECTIVE DATE UNTIL THE REGISTRANT SHALL FILE A FURTHER AMENDMENT WHICH SPECIFICALLY STATES THAT THIS REGISTRATION STATEMENT SHALL THEREAFTER BECOME EFFECTIVE IN ACCORDANCE WITH SECTION 8(A) OF THE SECURITIES ACT OF 1933 OR UNTIL THE REGISTRATION STATEMENT

SHALL BECOME EFFECTIVE ON SUCH DATE AS THE COMMISSION, ACTING PURSUANT TO SAID SECTION 8(A), MAY DETERMINE.

THE INFORMATION IN THIS PROSPECTUS IS NOT COMPLETE AND MAY BE CHANGED. WE MAY NOT SELL THESE SECURITIES UNTIL THE REGISTRATION STATEMENT FILED WITH THE SECURITIES AND EXCHANGE COMMISSION IS EFFECTIVE. THIS PROSPECTUS IS NOT AN OFFER TO SELL THESE SECURITIES AND IT IS NOT SOLICITING AN OFFER TO BUY THESE SECURITIES IN ANY STATE WHERE THE OFFER OR SALE IS NOT PERMITTED.

SUBJECT TO COMPLETION, DATED NOVEMBER 14, 2001

17,400,000 Shares

[LOGO]
Common Stock

The shares of common stock are being sold by the selling shareholders named in this prospectus. We will not receive any of the proceeds from the shares of common stock sold by the selling shareholders.

Prior to this offering, there has been no public market for our common stock. The initial public offering price of the common stock is expected to be between $23.00 and $25.00 per share. Our common stock has been authorized for listing on the New York Stock Exchange under the symbol "WTW."

The underwriters have an option to purchase a maximum of 2,610,000 additional shares from certain of the selling shareholders to cover over-allotments of shares.

Investing in our common stock involves risks. See "Risk Factors" beginning on page 8.

	Price to Public	Underwriting Discounts and Commissions	Proceeds to Selling Shareholders
Per Share	$	$	$
Total	$	$	$

Delivery of the shares of common stock will be made on or about 2001.

Neither the Securities and Exchange Commission nor any state securities commission has approved or disapproved of these securities or determined if this prospectus is truthful or complete. Any representation to the contrary is a criminal offense.

Credit Suisse First Boston   Goldman, Sachs & Co.

Merrill Lynch & Co.

Salomon Smith Barney   UBS Warburg

The date of this prospectus is _____.

Picture of Weight Watchers Magazine Cover
Picture of Classroom Meeting
Weight Watchers Logo
Picture of Program Materials
Picture of Program Materials
Picture of Woman Measuring Weight Loss
Picture of Woman Measuring Weight Loss
Picture of Spokeswoman at a Press Conference

TABLE OF CONTENTS

YOU SHOULD RELY ONLY ON THE INFORMATION CON-
TAINED IN THIS DOCUMENT OR TO WHICH WE HAVE REFERRED
YOU. WE HAVE NOT AUTHORIZED ANYONE TO PROVIDE YOU
WITH INFORMATION THAT IS DIFFERENT. THIS DOCUMENT
MAY BE USED ONLY WHERE IT IS LEGAL TO SELL THESE SECU-
RITIES. THE INFORMATION IN THIS DOCUMENT IS ACCURATE
ONLY ON THE DATE OF THIS DOCUMENT.

In this prospectus, "Weight Watchers," "we," "us" and "our" refer to
Weight Watchers International, Inc. and its subsidiaries, unless the context otherwise requires. We refer to our classroom operations that are run
directly by us as company-owned and those run by our franchisees as
franchised. Unless otherwise indicated, the information in this prospectus
assumes the completion of the 4.70536-for-one split of our common stock
that will occur prior to the completion of this offering.

In January 2001, we acquired the business of one of our two largest
franchisees, Weighco Enterprises, Inc. and its subsidiaries, which we
collectively refer to as Weighco. When we state that information is presented on a pro forma basis, we have taken into account the Weighco
acquisition on the pro forma basis described under "Pro Forma Combined Financial Information."

UNTIL _____, 2001 (25 DAYS AFTER THE COMMENCE-
MENT OF THE OFFERING), ALL DEALERS THAT EFFECT
TRANSACTIONS IN THESE SECURITIES, WHETHER OR NOT
PARTICIPATING IN THIS OFFERING, MAY BE REQUIRED TO
DELIVER A PROSPECTUS. THIS IS IN ADDITION TO THE
DEALER'S OBLIGATION TO DELIVER A PROSPECTUS WHEN
ACTING AS AN UNDERWRITER AND WITH RESPECT TO UNSOLD
ALLOTMENTS OR SUBSCRIPTIONS.

PROSPECTUS SUMMARY

THIS SUMMARY HIGHLIGHTS INFORMATION CONTAINED
ELSEWHERE IN THIS PROSPECTUS IS NOT COMPLETE AND MAY
NOT CONTAIN ALL THE INFORMATION THAT MAY BE IMPOR-
TANT TO YOU. YOU SHOULD READ THE ENTIRE PROSPEC-
TUS BEFORE MAKING AN INVESTMENT DECISION, ESPECIALLY
THE INFORMATION PRESENTED UNDER THE HEADING "RISK
FACTORS."

WEIGHT WATCHERS

We are a leading global branded consumer company and the leading provider of weight-loss services in 27 countries around the world. Our programs help people lose weight and maintain their weight loss and, as a result, improve their health, enhance their lifestyles and build self-confidence. At the core of our business are weekly meetings, which promote weight loss through education and group support in conjunction with a flexible, healthy diet. Each week more than one million members attend approximately 37,000 Weight Watchers meetings, which are run by over 13,000 classroom leaders. Our classroom leaders teach, inspire, motivate and act as role models for our members. Our members typically enroll to attend consecutive weekly meetings and have historically demonstrated a consistent re-enrollment pattern across many years.

We have experienced strong growth in sales and profits over the last five years since we made the strategic decision to re-focus our meetings exclusively on our group education approach. We discontinued the in-meeting sale of pre-packaged meals added in 1990 in our North America company-owned operations by our previous owner, Heinz. We also modernized our diet to adapt it to contemporary lifestyles. Through these initiatives, combined with our strengthened management and strategic focus since our acquisition by Artal Luxembourg, we have grown our attendance at a compound annual rate of approximately 13% from fiscal 1997 through 2000 and our operating profit margin improved from 6.7% (before a restructuring charge) to 25.9% over the same period. . . .

The number of overweight and obese people worldwide has been increasing due to improving living standards and changing eating patterns, as well as increasingly sedentary lifestyles. The proportion of U.S. adults who are overweight has grown from 47% to 61% over the last 20 years, and the number of overweight people worldwide now exceeds one billion. A growing number of overweight people are dieting not only because of a desire to improve their appearance but also due to a greater awareness of the health risks associated with being overweight.

Throughout our 40-year history, we have maintained that long-term behavior modification is the only effective way to achieve sustainable weight loss. Although approximately 70% of U.S. dieters try to lose weight by themselves, clinical studies have shown that people who attend Weight Watchers meetings are much more likely to lose weight than people who diet on their own. In contrast to our group education approach to long-term behavior modification, most weight-loss companies have focused on quick-fix methods, such as fad diets, meal replacements and diet drugs, and have typically experienced limited or short-lived success. We believe that our approach will continue to achieve success and that we will capture an increasing share of the growing worldwide market for weight-loss services.

OUR STRENGTHS

— BILLION DOLLAR GLOBAL BRAND. Our proven 40-year track record of safe and sensible weight loss has established WEIGHT WATCHERS as the leading global weight-loss brand. We believe that our brand conveys an image of effective, healthy and flexible weight loss in a supportive environment. Our brand is widely recognized throughout the world with retail sales of over $1.5 billion in 2000, including sales by licensees and franchisees. Currently, over 97% of U.S. women recognize the WEIGHT WATCHERS brand. . . .

— LEADING MARKET POSITION. We are the market leader in weight-loss services in every country in which we operate, other than Denmark, Poland and South Africa. . . .

— LOYAL MEMBER BASE. For many of our members, our classroom program is an inspirational experience that helps them address their life-long challenge of weight control. Our members have historically demonstrated a consistent pattern of repeat enrollment over a number of years. On average, in our North America company-owned, or NACO, operations, our members have enrolled in four separate program cycles.

— ATTRACTIVE VALUE TO MEMBERS. Our low meeting fees ($10 in our NACO operations) offer members an attractive value as compared to other alternatives. For their fee, our members gain access to our scientifically developed diet, detailed program materials and class instruction by one of our trained leaders, as well as group support where members contribute to each other's weight-loss success.

— UNIQUE BUSINESS MODEL. Our business model features high margins, a variable cost structure and low capital requirements.

— HIGH CONTRIBUTION MARGINS. During 2000, our meetings generated a contribution margin of approximately 50%. In that period, for example, our NACO meetings averaged attendance of 34 members and generated average revenues of over $440 per class, including product sales, while our cost of sales is primarily the compensation of two or three part-time employees, the hourly rental of the meeting location and the cost of products sold.

— VARIABLE COST STRUCTURE. Our staff is usually paid on a commission basis and space is typically rented as needed. Moreover, we adjust the number of meetings according to demand, including seasonal fluctuations. This variable cost structure enables us to maintain high margins across varying levels of demand.

— LOW MARKETING COSTS. Our marketing expenditures were less than 15% of our revenues in 2000. Our strong brand, together with the effectiveness of our program and our loyal member base, enable us to attract new and returning members efficiently through both word-of-mouth referrals and mass marketing programs.
— STRONG FREE CASH FLOW. In 2000, our operating income margin was over 25%, while our capital expenditures were less than 1% of revenues. Because we can add additional meetings with little or no capital expenditures and our members typically pay cash at each meeting or prepay for a series of meetings, we require little new capital to grow.

OUR GROWTH STRATEGY

The large and growing global weight-loss market provides us with significant growth potential. In addition, we believe we can increase our share of this market by:

— INCREASING PENETRATION IN EXISTING MAJOR MARKETS. In the United Kingdom, the penetration rate of our target demographic group, overweight women ages 25 to 64, by all group education-based commercial weight-loss programs now exceeds 20%. We believe that this demonstrates the potential for significant increases in penetration in our other major markets. Because we do not face significant group education-based competition outside the United Kingdom, we believe that we are best positioned to capture this growth. . . .
— DEVELOPING LESS PENETRATED MARKETS AND ENTERING NEW MARKETS. We believe that we have significant long-term growth opportunities in countries where we have established a meeting infrastructure but where our penetration rates are relatively low. For example, in Germany, we have grown attendance by over 65% in the twelve months ended September 29, 2001, while still penetrating less than 2% of our target market. . . .
— GROWING PRODUCT SALES. In 2000, sales of our proprietary products represented 26% of our revenues, up from 11% in fiscal 1997. We have grown our product sales per attendance by focusing on a core group of products that complement our program. We currently sell snack bars, books, CD-ROMs, POINTS calculators and other items primarily through classroom operations. We will continue to optimize our classroom product offerings by updating existing products and selectively introducing new products.
— GROWING LICENSING ROYALTIES. We currently license the WEIGHT WATCHERS brand in certain categories of food, apparel, books and other products. We derived less than 2% of our 2000 revenues from licensing and royalties but believe there are opportunities

to take fuller advantage of the strength of our brand through additional licensing agreements. . . .

— ADDRESSING NEW CUSTOMER SEGMENTS. We believe there are significant opportunities to expand our customer base by developing products and services designed to meet the needs of a broader audience. . . .

RECENT DEVELOPMENTS

On October 29, 2001, we reported net revenues for the three months and nine months ended September 29, 2001 of $144.0 million and $478.3 million, respectively. Our net revenues for the three months and nine months ended September 29, 2001 increased 19.4% and 25.2% compared with pro forma net revenues for the comparable prior year periods. Our operating income for the three months and nine months ended September 29, 2001 was $50.9 million and $160.0 million, respectively. Our operating income for the three months and nine months ended September 29, 2001 increased 63.5% and 46.5% compared with pro forma operating income for the comparable prior year periods.

The increases in our revenues and profitability reflect the continuing strong growth in attendance and product sales across our major markets. Attendance was 10.8 million for the quarter ended September 29, 2001, an increase from pro forma attendance of 9.1 million for the three months ended September 30, 2000. . . .

We are a Virginia corporation incorporated in 1974. Our principal executive offices are located at 175 Crossways Park West, Woodbury, New York 11797-2055. Our telephone number at that address is (516) 390-1400.

THE OFFERING

Common stock offered by the selling shareholders	17,400,000 shares (or 20,010,000 shares if the underwriters exercise the over-allotment option in full)
Total common stock outstanding after this offering	105,407,142 shares
Use of proceeds	We will not receive any of the proceeds from the sale of shares by the selling shareholders. The selling shareholders will receive all net proceeds from the sale of shares of our common stock offered in this prospectus.
Dividend policy	We do not expect to pay any dividends on our common stock for the foreseeable future.
New York Stock Exchange symbol.	WTW

The number of shares of common stock shown to be outstanding after this offering is based on the number of shares outstanding as of September 29, 2001. This number excludes:

— 5,763,692 shares of our common stock issuable upon exercise of outstanding stock options and

— 1,294,348 shares of our common stock reserved for future issuance under our existing stock option plan.

SUMMARY PRO FORMA COMBINED FINANCIAL INFORMATION

The summary pro forma combined financial information has been derived from the unaudited pro forma combined statements of operations and the related note included elsewhere in this prospectus, which give effect to our acquisition on January 16, 2001 of the franchised territories and certain business assets of Weighco for $83.8 million and the related financing of the acquisition. We financed the acquisition with available cash of $23.8 million and additional borrowings of $60.0 million under our senior credit facilities. . . .

Effective April 30, 2000, we changed our fiscal year end from the last Saturday in April to the Saturday closest to December 31. As a result of this change in our reporting period, the significant growth in our business since the fiscal year ended April 29, 2000 and the Weighco acquisition, we have included unaudited pro forma combined results of operations for the twelve months ended December 30, 2000. Given these events, we believe the pro forma results of operations for the twelve months ended December 30, 2000 are more indicative of our current operations. Our results of operations for the twelve months ended December 30, 2000 have been derived from our historical results for the eight months ended December 30, 2000, plus our results for the four months ended April 29, 2000, which are derived from our results for the historical fiscal year ended April 29, 2000. We have included a comparison of the nine months ended September 29, 2001 to the nine months ended October 28, 2000, which, in the opinion of our management, is the available period most comparable to the nine months ended September 29, 2001.

SUMMARY PRO FORMA COMBINED FINANCIAL INFORMATION

	FISCAL YEAR ENDED APRIL 29, 2000	TWELVE MONTHS ENDED DECEMBER 30, 2000	NINE MONTHS ENDED	
			OCTOBER 28, 2000	SEPTEMBER 29, 2001
	(53 weeks)	(54 weeks)	(40 weeks)	(39 weeks)
		(in millions, except per share amounts)		
STATEMENT OF OPERATIONS INFORMATION:				
Revenues, net	$436.4	$488.2	$382.1	$480.1
Cost of revenues	216.8	237.5	183.3	215.6
Gross profit	219.6	250.7	198.8	264.5
Marketing expenses	55.0	58.9	40.3	51.8
Selling, general and administrative expenses	60.3	62.7	49.3	51.9
Transaction costs	8.3	—	—	—
Operating income	96.0	129.1	109.2	160.8
Interest expense, net	40.1	66.8	49.9	42.3
Other (income) expense, net	(10.5)	7.6	(6.7)	13.9
Income before income taxes and minority interest	66.4	54.7	66.0	104.6
Provision for income taxes	28.1	20.1	21.3	38.8
Income before minority interest.	38.3	34.6	44.7	65.8
Minority interest	0.8	0.3	0.2	0.1
Net income	$ 37.5	$ 34.3	$ 44.5	$ 65.7
Preferred stock dividends	$ 0.9	$ 1.5	$ 1.1	$ 1.1
Net income available to common shareholders	$ 36.6	$ 32.8	$ 43.4	$ 64.6
PER SHARE INFORMATION:				
Basic earnings per share	0.20	0.29	0.39	0.59
Diluted earnings per share	0.20	0.29	0.39	0.58
Basic weighted average number of shares*	182.1	112.0	112.0	109.8
Diluted weighted average number of shares*	182.1	112.0	112.0	111.4
OTHER FINANCIAL INFORMATION:				
Depreciation and amortization ..	18.1	14.0	11.5	10.0
Capital expenditures	2.7	4.3	2.7	1.9

* Prior to our acquisition by Artal Luxembourg on September 29, 1999, there were 4,705 shares of our common stock outstanding. In connection with the transactions related to our acquisition, we declared a stock split that resulted in 276,428,607 outstanding shares of our common stock. We have adjusted our historical statements to reflect the stock split. We then repurchased 164,441,039 shares in connection with the transactions so that upon completion of our acquisition, there were 111,987,568 shares of our common stock outstanding.

SUMMARY HISTORICAL
CONSOLIDATED FINANCIAL INFORMATION

The following table sets forth certain of our historical financial information. The summary historical consolidated financial information as of and for the fiscal years ended April 25, 1998, April 24, 1999 and April 29, 2000 and the eight months ended December 30, 2000 have been derived from, and should be read in conjunction with, our audited consolidated financial statements and the related notes included elsewhere in this prospectus. The summary historical consolidated financial information as of and for the nine months ended October 28, 2000 and September 29, 2001 have been derived from, and should be read in conjunction with, our unaudited consolidated financial statements and the related notes included elsewhere in this prospectus. Interim results for the nine months ended September 29, 2001 are not necessarily indicative of, and are not projections for, the results to be expected for the full fiscal year.

	FISCAL YEAR ENDED			EIGHT MONTHS ENDED	NINE MONTHS ENDED	
	APRIL 25, 1998	APRIL 24, 1999	APRIL 29, 2000	DEC. 30, 2000	OCT. 28, 2000	SEPT. 29, 2001
	(52 weeks)	(52 weeks)	(53 weeks)	(35 weeks)	(40 weeks)	(39 weeks)
			(in millions, except per share amounts)			
STATEMENT OF OPERATIONS INFORMATION:						
Revenues, net	$297.2	$364.6	$399.5	$273.2	$343.5	$478.3
Cost of revenues	160.0	178.9	201.4	139.3	167.2	215.1
Gross profit	137.2	185.7	198.1	133.9	176.3	263.2
Marketing expenses	49.2	52.9	51.5	27.0	37.1	51.5
Selling, general and administrative expenses	44.1	48.9	50.7	32.2	40.8	51.7
Transaction costs	—	—	8.3	—	—	—
Operating income	43.9	83.9	87.6	74.7	98.4	160.0
Interest (income) expense, net	(4.9)	(7.1)	31.1	37.1	42.9	42.0
Other expense (income), net	4.3	5.2	(10.4)	16.5	(6.7)	13.9
Income before income taxes and minority interest	44.5	85.8	66.9	21.1	62.2	104.1
Provision for income taxes	19.9	36.4	28.3	5.9	19.9	38.6
Income before minority interest	24.6	49.4	38.6	15.2	42.3	65.5
Minority interest	0.8	1.5	0.8	0.2	0.2	0.1
Net income	$ 23.8	$ 47.9	$ 37.8	$ 15.0	$ 42.1	$ 65.4
Preferred stock dividends	—	—	$ 0.9	$ 1.0	$ 1.1	$ 1.1
Net income available to common shareholders	$ 23.8	$ 47.9	$ 36.9	$ 14.0	$ 41.0	$ 64.3

PER SHARE INFORMATION:

Basic earnings per share	$ 0.09	$ 0.17	$ ·0.20	$ 0.13	$ 0.37	$ 0.59
Diluted earnings per share	$ 0.09	$ 0.17	$ 0.20	$ 0.13	$ 0.37	$ 0.58
Basic weighted average number of shares*	276.2	276.2	182.1	112.0	112.0	109.8
Diluted weighted average number of shares*	276.2	276.2	182.1	112.0	112.0	111.4

OTHER FINANCIAL INFORMATION:
Net cash provided by (used in):

Operating activities	$ 36.4	$ 57.9	$ 49.9	$ 28.9	$ 50.1	$ 120.2
Investing activities	(4.9)	(3.0)	(19.6)	(21.6)	(15.7)	(110.7)
Financing activities	(30.6)	(47.7)	8.1	(8.0)	(4.7)	(15.5)
Depreciation and amortization ...	8.8	9.6	10.4	7.9	8.5	9.8
Capital expenditures	3.4	2.5	1.9	3.6	2.2	1.9

BALANCE SHEET INFORMATION
(AT END OF PERIOD):

Working capital (deficit)	$ 65.8	$ 91.2	$ (0.9)	$ 10.2	$ 3.3	$ (35.2)
Total assets	370.8	371.4	334.2	346.2	346.9	423.4
Total debt	41.1	39.6	474.6	470.7	460.5	480.8
Redeemable securities:						
Preferred stock	—	—	25.9	26.0	25.7	25.6

*Prior to our acquisition by Artal Luxembourg on September 29,1999, there were 4,705 shares of our common stock outstanding. In connection with the transactions related to our acquisition, we declared a stock split that resulted in 276,428,607 outstanding shares of our common stock. We have adjusted our historical statements to reflect the stock split. We then repurchased 164,441,039 shares in connection with the transactions so that upon completion of our acquisition, there were 111,987,568 shares of our common stock outstanding.

RISK FACTORS

AN INVESTMENT IN OUR COMMON STOCK INVOLVES RISKS. YOU SHOULD CONSIDER CAREFULLY, IN ADDITION TO THE OTHER INFORMATION CONTAINED IN THIS PROSPECTUS, THE FOLLOWING RISK FACTORS BEFORE DECIDING TO PURCHASE ANY SHARES OF OUR COMMON STOCK.

RISKS RELATING TO OUR COMPANY

COMPETITION FROM A VARIETY OF OTHER WEIGHT-LOSS METHODS COULD RESULT IN DECREASED DEMAND FOR OUR SERVICES.

The weight-loss business is highly competitive and we compete against a large number of alternative providers of various sizes, some of which may have greater financial resources than we. We compete against self-administered weight-loss regimens, other commercial weight-loss programs, Internet-based weight-loss programs, nutritionists, dietitians, the pharmaceutical industry, dietary supplements and certain government agencies and non-profit groups that offer weight control help by means of diets, exercise and weight-loss drugs. We also compete against food manufacturers and distributors that are developing and marketing meal replacement and diet products to weight-conscious consumers. In addition, new or different products or methods of weight control are continually being introduced. This competition and any increase in competition, including new pharmaceuticals and other technological and scientific developments in weight control, may result in decreased demand for our services.

OUR OPERATING RESULTS DEPEND ON THE EFFECTIVENESS OF OUR MARKETING AND ADVERTISING PROGRAMS.

Our business success depends on our ability to attract new members to our classes and retain existing members. The effectiveness of our marketing practices, in particular our advertising campaigns, is important to our financial performance. . . .

IF WE DO NOT CONTINUE TO DEVELOP NEW PRODUCTS AND SERVICES AND ENHANCE OUR EXISTING PRODUCTS AND SER-VICES, OUR BUSINESS MAY SUFFER.

Our future success depends on our ability to continue to develop and market new products and services and to enhance our existing products and services on a timely basis to respond to new and evolving customer demands, achieve market acceptance and keep pace with new nutritional and weight-loss developments. We may not be successful in developing, introducing on a timely basis or marketing any new or enhanced products and services, and we cannot assure you that any new or enhanced products or services will be accepted by the market. . . .

OUR DEBT SERVICE OBLIGATIONS COULD IMPEDE OUR OPERATIONS AND FLEXIBILITY.

Our financial performance could be affected by our level of debt. As of September 29, 2001, we had total debt and redeemable preferred stock of $506.4 million. . . . Our net interest expense for the eight months ended December 30, 2000 and for the nine months ended September 29, 2001 was $37.1 million and $42.0 million, respectively.

Our level of debt could have important consequences for you, including the following:

— we will need to use a large portion of the money we earn to pay principal and interest on outstanding amounts due . . . which will reduce the amount of money available to us for financing our operations and other business activities,

— we may have a much higher level of debt than certain of our competitors, which may put us at a competitive disadvantage,

— we may have difficulty borrowing money in the future and

— our debt level makes us more vulnerable to economic downturns and adverse developments in our business. . . .

WE ARE SUBJECT TO RESTRICTIVE DEBT COVENANTS, WHICH MAY RESTRICT OUR OPERATIONAL FLEXIBILITY.

Our senior credit facilities contain covenants that restrict our ability to incur additional indebtedness, pay dividends on and redeem capital stock, make other restricted payments, including investments, sell our assets and enter into consolidations, mergers and transfers of all or substantially all of our assets. Our senior credit facilities also require us to maintain specified financial ratios and satisfy financial condition tests. These tests and financial ratios become more restrictive over the life of the credit facilities. Our ability to meet those financial ratios and tests can be affected by events beyond our control and we cannot assure you that we will meet those ratios and tests. A breach of any of these covenants, ratios, tests or restrictions could result in an event of default under the credit facilities. In an event of default under the credit facilities, the lenders could elect to declare all amounts outstanding thereunder to be immediately due and payable. If the lenders under the credit facilities accelerate the payment of the indebtedness, we cannot assure you that our assets would be sufficient to repay in full that indebtedness and our other indebtedness that would become due as a result of any acceleration. . . .

ACTIONS TAKEN BY OUR FRANCHISEES AND LICENSEES MAY HARM OUR BRAND OR REPUTATION.

We believe that the WEIGHT WATCHERS brand is one of our most valuable assets and that our reputation provides us with a competitive advantage. . . . Because our franchisees and licensees are independent third parties with their own financial objectives, actions taken by them, including breaches of their contractual obligations, such as not following our diets or not maintaining our quality standards, could harm our brand or reputation. Also, the products we license to third parties may be subject to product recalls or other deficiencies. Any negative publicity associated with these actions or recalls may adversely affect our reputation and thereby result in decreased classroom attendance and lower revenues.

DISPUTES WITH OUR FRANCHISE OPERATORS COULD DIVERT OUR MANAGEMENT'S ATTENTION.

In the past, we have had disputes with our franchisees regarding operations and revenue sharing. We continue to have disputes with a few of our franchisees. . . . These disputes and any future disputes could divert the attention of our management from their ordinary responsibilities.

OUR INTERNATIONAL OPERATIONS EXPOSE US TO ECONOMIC, POLITICAL AND SOCIAL RISKS IN THE COUNTRIES IN WHICH WE OPERATE.

The international nature of our existing and planned operations involves a number of risks, including changes in U.S. and foreign government regulations, tariffs, taxes and exchange controls, economic downturns, inflation and political and social instability in the countries in which we operate and our dependence on foreign personnel. . . .

WE ARE EXPOSED TO FOREIGN CURRENCY RISKS FROM OUR INTERNATIONAL OPERATIONS THAT COULD ADVERSELY AFFECT OUR FINANCIAL RESULTS.

A significant portion of our revenues and operating costs are, and a portion of our indebtedness is, denominated in foreign currencies. We are therefore exposed to fluctuations in the exchange rates between the U.S. dollar and the currencies in which our foreign operations receive revenues and pay expenses, including debt service. . . .

OUR RESULTS OF OPERATIONS MAY DECLINE AS A RESULT OF A DOWNTURN IN GENERAL ECONOMIC CONDITIONS.

. . . A downturn in general economic conditions or consumer confidence and spending in any of our major markets caused by the recent terrorist attacks or other events outside of our control could result in people curtailing their discretionary spending, which, in turn, could reduce attendance at our meetings. . . .

THE SEASONAL NATURE OF OUR BUSINESS COULD CAUSE OUR OPERATING RESULTS TO FLUCTUATE.

We have experienced and expect to continue to experience fluctuations in our quarterly results of operations. . . . This seasonality could cause our share price to fluctuate as the results of an interim financial period may not be indicative of our full year results. In addition, our classroom operations are subject to local conditions beyond our control, including the weather, natural disasters and other extraordinary events, that may prevent current or prospective members from attending or joining classes. . . .

OUR ADVERTISING AND FRANCHISE OPERATIONS ARE SUBJECT TO LEGISLATIVE AND REGULATORY RESTRICTIONS.

A number of laws and regulations govern our advertising, franchise operations and relations with consumers. The Federal Trade Commission, or FTC, and certain states regulate advertising, disclosures to consumers and franchisees and other consumer matters. Our customers may file actions on their own behalf, as a class or otherwise, and may file complaints with the FTC or state or local consumer affairs offices and these agencies may take action on their own initiative or on a referral from consumers or others.

During the mid-1990s, the FTC filed complaints against a number of commercial weight-loss providers alleging violations of the Federal Trade Commission Act by the use and content of advertisements for weight-loss programs that featured testimonials, claims for program success and safety and statements as to program costs to participants. In 1997, we entered into a consent order with the FTC settling all contested issues raised in the complaint filed against us. The consent order requires us to comply with certain procedures and disclosures in connection with our advertisements of products and services. . . .

RISKS RELATED TO THIS OFFERING

THERE IS NO EXISTING MARKET FOR OUR COMMON STOCK, AND WE DO NOT KNOW IF ONE WILL DEVELOP TO PROVIDE YOU WITH ADEQUATE LIQUIDITY.

There has not been a public market for our common stock. We cannot predict the extent to which investor interest in our company will lead to the development of a trading market on the New York Stock Exchange or otherwise or how liquid that market might become. The initial public offering price for the shares will be determined by negotiations between the selling shareholders and the representatives of the underwriters and may not be indicative of prices that will prevail in the open market following this offering.

ARTAL LUXEMBOURG CONTROLS US AND MAY HAVE CONFLICTS OF INTEREST WITH OTHER SHAREHOLDERS IN THE FUTURE.

Artal Luxembourg S.A. controls us. After this offering, Artal Luxembourg will beneficially own 78.8% of our common stock or 76.4% if the underwriters exercise their over-allotment option in full. As a result, Artal Luxembourg will continue to be able to control the election and removal of our directors and determine our corporate and management policies, including potential mergers or acquisitions, payment of dividends, asset sales and other significant corporate transactions. We cannot assure you that the interests of Artal Luxembourg will coincide with the interests of other holders of our common stock. In addition, Artal Luxembourg also owns 72.3% of the common stock, or 48.1% on a fully diluted basis, of our licensee, WeightWatchers.com. Artal Luxembourg's interests with respect to WeightWatchers.com may differ from the interests of our other shareholders.

FUTURE SALES OF OUR SHARES COULD DEPRESS THE MARKET PRICE OF OUR COMMON STOCK.

The market price of our common stock could decline as a result of sales of a large number of shares of our common stock in the market after this offering or the perception that these sales could occur. . . .

Following this offering, Artal Luxembourg will own 83,062,423 shares of our common stock or 80,517,663 shares if the underwriters exercise their over-allotment option in full. Artal Luxembourg will be able to sell its shares in the public market from time to time, subject to certain limitations on the timing, amount and method of those sales imposed by SEC regulations. Artal Luxembourg and the underwriters have agreed to a "lock-up" period, meaning that Artal Luxembourg may not sell any of its shares without the prior consent of Credit Suisse First Boston Corporation for 180 days after the date of this prospectus. Artal Luxembourg has the right to cause us to register the sale of shares of common stock owned by it and to include its shares in future registration statements relating to our securities. If Artal Luxembourg were to sell a large number of its shares, the market price of our stock could decline significantly. In addition, the perception in the public markets that sales by Artal Luxembourg might occur could also adversely affect the market price of our common stock.

In addition to Artal Luxembourg's lock-up period, sales of our common stock are also restricted by lock-up agreements that our directors and executive officers and the selling shareholders have entered into with the underwriters. . . .

OUR ARTICLES OF INCORPORATION AND BYLAWS AND VIRGINIA CORPORATE LAW CONTAIN PROVISIONS THAT MAY DISCOURAGE A TAKEOVER ATTEMPT.

Provisions contained in our articles of incorporation and bylaws and the laws of Virginia, the state in which we are organized, could make it more difficult for a third party to acquire us, even if doing so might be beneficial to our shareholders. . . . For example, our articles of incorporation authorize our board of directors to determine the rights, preferences, privileges and restrictions of unissued series of preferred stock, without any vote or action by our shareholders. Thus, our board of directors can authorize and issue shares of preferred stock with voting or conversion rights that could adversely affect the voting or other rights of holders of our common stock. . . .

THE MARKET PRICE OF OUR COMMON STOCK MAY BE VOLATILE, WHICH COULD CAUSE THE VALUE OF YOUR INVESTMENT TO DECLINE.

Securities markets worldwide experience significant price and volume fluctuations. . . . In addition, our operating results could be below the expectations of public market analysts and investors, and in response, the market price of our common stock could decrease significantly. You may be unable to resell your shares of our common stock at or above the initial public offering price.

CAUTIONARY NOTICE
REGARDING FORWARD-LOOKING STATEMENTS

This prospectus includes forward-looking statements including, in particular, the statements about our plans, strategies and prospects under the headings "Prospectus Summary," "Management's Discussion and Analysis of Financial Condition and Results of Operations," "Industry" and "Business." We have used the words "may," "will," "expect," "antic-ipate," "believe," "estimate," "plan," "intend" and similar expressions in this prospectus to identify forward-looking statements. . . . Actual results could differ materially from those projected in the forward-looking statements. These forward-looking statements are subject to risks, uncertainties and assumptions, including, among other things:

— competition, including price competition and competition with self-help, medical and other weight-loss programs and products;
— risks associated with the relative success of our marketing and advertising;
— risks associated with the continued attractiveness of our programs;
— risks associated with our ability to meet our obligations related to our outstanding indebtedness;
— risks associated with general economic conditions;
— adverse results in litigation and regulatory matters, the adoption of adverse legislation or regulations, more aggressive enforce-ment of existing legislation or regulations or a change in the interpretation of existing legislation or regulations; and
— the other factors referenced under the heading "Risk Factors."

You should not put undue reliance on any forward-looking state-ments. You should understand that many important factors, including those discussed under the headings "Risk Factors" and "Management's Discussion and Analysis of Financial Conditions and Results of Opera-tions," could cause our results to differ materially from those expressed or suggested in any forward-looking statements.

USE OF PROCEEDS

We will not receive any of the proceeds from the sale of shares by the selling shareholders. The selling shareholders will receive all net proceeds from the sale of the shares of our common stock in this offering.

DIVIDEND POLICY

We do not intend to pay any dividends on our common stock in the foreseeable future. . . .

CAPITALIZATION

The following table sets forth our cash and our capitalization as of September 29, 2001. You should read this table in conjunction with our consolidated financial statements and the related notes included elsewhere in this prospectus. . . .

SEPTEMBER 29, 2001

	(in millions)
Cash	$ 37.9
Long-term debt (including current maturities):	
Senior credit facilities	$ 239.6
Senior subordinated notes due 2009	241.2
Total long-term debt	480.8
Redeemable preferred stock	25.6
Shareholders' deficit:	
Common stock, no par value (1,000,000,000 authorized, 111,987,568 issued and 105,407,142 outstanding	—
Treasury stock, at cost, 6,580,426 shares	(26.6)
Accumulated (deficit)	(152.2)
Accumulated other comprehensive (loss)	(15.3)
Total shareholders' (deficit)	(194.1)
Total capitalization	$ 312.3

PRO FORMA COMBINED FINANCIAL INFORMATION

On January 16, 2001, we acquired the franchised territories and certain business assets, including inventory, property and equipment, of Weighco for $83.8 million. . . . The acquisition has been accounted for under the purchase method of accounting and, accordingly, the results of operations of Weighco are included from the date of acquisition. . . .

The unaudited pro forma combined statements of operations give effect to the Weighco acquisition and the related financing as if each had occurred on April 25, 1999. . . .

Effective April 30, 2000, we changed our fiscal year end from the last Saturday in April to the Saturday closest to December 31. As a result of this change in our reporting period, the significant growth in our business since the fiscal year ended April 29, 2000 and the Weighco acquisition, we have included unaudited pro forma combined results of operations for the twelve months ended December 30, 2000. Given these events, we believe the pro forma results of operations for the twelve months ended December 30, 2000 are more indicative of our current operations. We have included a comparison of the nine months ended September 29, 2001 to the nine months ended October 28, 2000, which, in the opinion of our management, is the available period most comparable to the nine months ended September 29, 2001. . . .

PRO FORMA COMBINED STATEMENT OF OPERATIONS FOR THE TWELVE MONTHS ENDED DECEMBER 30, 2000 (UNAUDITED)

[Pro Forma Statements Omitted: eds.]

SELECTED HISTORICAL FINANCIAL AND OTHER INFORMATION

The following table sets forth our selected historical financial and other information and the related notes. . . .

	FISCAL YEAR ENDED				
	APRIL 27, 1996 (52 weeks)	APRIL 26, 1997 (52 weeks)	APRIL 25, 1998 (52 weeks)	APRIL 24, 1999 (52 weeks)	APRIL 29, 2000 (53 weeks)
	(in millions, except per share amounts)				
STATEMENT OF OPERATIONS INFORMATION:					
Revenues, net	$ 323.3	$ 292.8	$ 297.2	$ 364.6	$ 399.5
Cost of revenues..........................	190.9	230.4(1)	160.0	178.9	201.4
Gross profit	132.4	62.4	137.2	185.7	198.1
Marketing expenses	53.9	48.9	49.2	52.9	51.5
Selling, general and administrative expenses	51.9	45.5(1)	44.1	48.9	50.7
Transaction costs	—	—	—	—	8.3
Operating income (loss)	26.6	(32.0)	43.9	83.9	87.6
Interest expense (income), net	3.3	1.0	(4.9)	(7.1)	31.1
Other expense (income), net	4.8	3.3	4.3	5.2	(10.4)
Income (loss) before income taxes and minority interests	18.5	(36.3)	44.5	85.8	66.9
(Benefit from) provision for income taxes...	(3.6)	(12.9)	19.9	36.4	28.3
Income (loss) before minority interests ...	22.1	(23.4)	24.6	49.4	38.6
Minority interest	0.6	0.6	0.8	1.5	0.8
Net income (loss)	$ 21.5	$ (24.0)	$ 23.8	$ 47.9	$ 37.8
Preferred stock dividends	—	—	—	—	$ 0.9
Net income (loss) available to common shareholders	$ 21.5	$ (24.0)	$ 23.8	147.9	$ 36.9

[Schedule of 8 Month and 9 Month Financial Performance Omitted: eds.]

MANAGEMENT'S DISCUSSION AND ANALYSIS OF FINANCIAL CONDITION AND RESULTS OF OPERATIONS

YOU SHOULD READ THE FOLLOWING DISCUSSION IN CONJUNCTION WITH "SELECTED HISTORICAL FINANCIAL AND OTHER INFORMATION" AND OUR CONSOLIDATED FINANCIAL STATEMENTS AND RELATED NOTES INCLUDED ELSEWHERE IN THIS PROSPECTUS. UNLESS OTHERWISE NOTED, REFERENCES TO THE 1997, 1998, 1999 AND 2000 FISCAL YEARS ARE TO OUR FISCAL YEARS ENDED APRIL 26, 1997, APRIL 25, 1998, APRIL 24, 1999 AND APRIL 29, 2000, RESPECTIVELY. AFTER THE FISCAL YEAR ENDED APRIL 29, 2000, WE CHANGED OUR FISCAL YEAR END TO THE SATURDAY CLOSEST TO DECEMBER 31. ACCORDINGLY, THE FISCAL YEAR ENDED DECEMBER 30, 2000 IS AN EIGHT-MONTH PERIOD.

OVERVIEW

We are the leading provider of weight-loss services in 27 countries around the world. We conduct our business through a combination of company-owned and franchise operations, with company-owned operations accounting for 65% of total worldwide attendance in the first nine months of 2001. For the first nine months of 2001, 63% of our revenues were derived from our U.S. operations, and the remaining 37% of our revenues were derived from our international operations. We derive our revenues principally from:

— MEETING FEES. . . .
— PRODUCT SALES. . . .
— FRANCHISE ROYALTIES. . . .
— OTHER. We license our brand for certain foods, clothing, books and other products. We also generate revenues from the publishing of books and magazines and third-party advertising.

The following graph sets forth our revenues by category for the 1996, 1997, 1998, 1999 and 2000 fiscal years.

[Table Omitted: eds.]

— ACCELERATED GROWTH IN CONTINENTAL EUROPE. In Continental Europe, we have accelerated growth by adapting our business model to local conditions, implementing more aggressive marketing programs tailored to the local markets. . . . Attendance in our Continental Europe operations increased by 79% to 7.0 million in 2000 from 3.9 million in fiscal 1997.
— INCREASED PRODUCT SALES. We have increased our product sales by 265% from fiscal 1997 to 2000 by introducing new products and optimizing our product mix. . . .

Our worldwide attendance has grown by 55% in our company-owned operations from 23.0 million in fiscal 1997 to 35.7 million in 2000, and our operating profit margin has grown from 6.7% (before a restructuring charge) in fiscal 1997 to 25.9% in 2000.

ATTENDANCE IN COMPANY-OWNED OPERATIONS
(in millions)

[Table Omitted: eds.]

RESULTS OF OPERATIONS

The following table summarizes our historical income from operations as a percentage of revenues for the fiscal years ended April 25, 1998, April 24, 1999 and April 29, 2000, the eight months ended December 30, 2000 and the nine months ended October 28, 2000 and September 29, 2001.

| | FISCAL YEAR ENDED | | | EIGHT MONTHS ENDED | NINE MONTHS ENDED | |
	APRIL 25, 1998	APRIL 24, 1999	APRIL 29, 2000	DEC. 30, 2000	OCT. 28, 2000	SEPT. 29, 2001
Total revenues, net	100.0%	100.0%	100.0%	100.0%	100.0%	100.0%
Cost of revenues	53.8	49.1	50.4	51.0	48.7	45.0
Gross profit	46.2	50.9	49.6	49.0	51.3	55.0
Marketing expenses	16.6	14.5	12.9	9.9	10.8	10.8
Selling, general and administrative expenses	14.8	13.4	12.7	11.8	11.9	10.8
Operating income	14.8%	23.0%	24.0%	27.3%	28.6%	33.4%

COMPARISON OF THE NINE MONTHS ENDED SEPTEMBER 29, 2001 (39 WEEKS) TO THE NINE MONTHS ENDED OCTOBER 28, 2000 (40 WEEKS).

The nine months ended October 28, 2000, is, in the opinion of management, the available period most comparable to the nine months ended September 29, 2001.

[Five Page Narrative of the Above Omitted: eds.]

LIQUIDITY AND CAPITAL RESOURCES

During the eight months ended December 30, 2000 and for the nine months ended September 29, 2001, our primary source of funds to meet working capital needs was cash from operations. For the eight months ended December 30, 2000 cash flows provided by operating activities were $28.9 million. Cash and cash equivalents increased $0.5 million to $44.5 million during the eight months ended December 30, 2000. For the eight months ended December 30, 2000, cash flows provided by operating activities of $28.9 million were used primarily to fund a loan of $16.8 million to WeightWatchers.com and to repay principal on our outstanding senior credit facilities of $7.1 million. . . .

We believe that cash flows from operating activities, together with borrowings available under our revolving credit facility, will be sufficient for the next twelve months to fund currently anticipated capital expenditure requirements, debt service requirements and working capital expenditure requirements. Any future acquisitions, joint ventures or other similar transactions will likely require additional capital and we cannot be certain that any additional capital will be available on acceptable terms or at all. . . .

Our senior credit facilities contain covenants that restrict our ability to incur additional indebtedness, pay dividends on and redeem capital stock, make other restricted payments, including investments, sell our assets and enter into consolidations, mergers and transfers of all or substantially all of our assets. Our senior credit facilities also require us to maintain specified financial ratios and satisfy financial condition tests. These tests and financial ratios become more restrictive over the life of the senior credit facilities. . . .

In addition, we have one million shares of Series A Preferred Stock issued and outstanding with a preference value of $25.0 million. Holders of the Series A Preferred Stock are entitled to receive dividends at an annual rate of 6% payable annually in arrears. If there is a liquidation, dissolution or winding up, the holders of shares of Series A Preferred Stock are entitled to be paid out of our assets available for distribution to shareholders an amount in cash equal to the $25 liquidation preference per share plus all accrued and unpaid dividends prior to the distribution of any assets to holders of shares of our common stock. Subject to the restrictions set forth in our debt instruments, holders of our Series A Preferred Stock will have the right to cause us to repurchase their shares upon completion of this offering. If we are required to repurchase the Series A Preferred Stock, we expect that we would finance the purchase with our available cash or borrowings under our revolving credit facility. . . .

SEASONALITY

Our business is seasonal, with revenues generally decreasing at year end and during the summer months. Our advertising schedule supports the three key enrollment-generating seasons of the year: winter, spring and fall. Due to the timing of our marketing expenditures, particularly the higher level of expenditures in the first quarter, our operating income for the second quarter is generally the strongest, with the fourth quarter being the weakest.

The following table summarizes our historical quarterly results of operations for the periods indicated. We believe this presentation illustrates the seasonal nature of our business.

	HISTORICAL QUARTER ENDED						
				TWO MONTHS ENDED			
	APRIL 29, 2000	JULY 29, 2000	OCT. 28, 2000	DEC. 30, 2000	MARCH 31, 2001	JUNE 30, 2001	SEPT. 29, 2001
	(14 weeks)	(13 weeks)	(13 weeks)	(9 weeks) (in millions)	(13 weeks)	(13 weeks)	(13 weeks)
Revenues, net	$132.8	$103.1	$107.6	$62.5	$172.0	$162.3	$144.0
Gross profit	70.0	54.8	51.5	27.6	94.6	90.6	78.0
Marketing expenses	18.6	6.7	11.8	8.5	27.1	13.5	10.9
Selling, general and administrative							
expenses	17.2	11.5	12.0	8.7	17.7	17.8	16.2
Operating income	34.2	36.6	27.7	10.4	49.8	59.3	50.9
Net income (loss)	17.5	13.7	10.9	(9.6)	23.2	26.1	16.1·

As a result of the Weighco acquisition, we believe the following table summarizing our pro forma quarterly results of operations is more indicative of the impact of seasonality on our business than our historical quarterly results of operations.

	PROFORMA QUARTER ENDED				HISTORICAL QUARTER ENDED		
				TWO MONTHS ENDED			
	APRIL 29, 2000	JULY 29, 2000	OCT. 28, 2000	DEC. 30, 2000	MARCH 31, 2001	JUNE 30, 2001	SEPT. 29, 2001
	(14 weeks)	(13 weeks)	(13 weeks)	(9 weeks) (in millions)	(13 weeks)	(13 weeks)	(13 weeks)
Revenues, net	$145.4	$116.1	$120.6	$69.8	$173.8	$162.3	$144.0
Gross profit	77.9	62.1	58.8	319	95.9	90.6	78.0
Marketing expenses	20.1	7.4	12.8	8.8	27.4	13.5	10.9
Selling, general and administrative							
expenses	20.1	14.3	14.9	10.6	17.9	17.8	16.2
Operating income	37.7	40.4	31.1	12.5	50.6	59.3	50.9
Net income (loss)	18.4	14.5	11.6	(9.2)	23.5	26.1	16.1

Effective April 30, 2000, we changed our fiscal year end from the last Saturday in April to the Saturday closest to December 31. As a result of the change in our reporting period, beginning in 2001, we believe that our first quarter will typically have the highest revenue, followed by the second, third and fourth quarters, respectively.

ACCOUNTING STANDARDS

In July 2001, the Financial Accounting Standards Board issued Statement of Financial Accounting Standards, or SFAS, No. 141, "Business Combinations," and SFAS No.142, "Goodwill and Other Intangible Assets." SFAS 141 requires that all business combinations initiated after June 30, 2001 be accounted for by the purchase method of accounting. SFAS 142 specifies that goodwill and indefinite-lived intangible assets will no longer be amortized, but instead will be subject to annual impairment testing. We will adopt SFAS 142 on December 30, 2001. We are currently evaluating the effect that implementation of the new standards will have on our financial position, results of operations and cash flows.

QUANTITATIVE AND QUALITATIVE DISCLOSURES ABOUT MARKET RISK

We are exposed to foreign currency fluctuations and interest rate changes. . . .

    We enter into forward and swap contracts to hedge transactions denominated in foreign currencies to reduce the currency risk associated with fluctuating exchange rates. These contracts are used primarily to hedge certain intercompany cash flows and for payments arising from some of our foreign currency denominated obligations. Realized and unrealized gains and losses from these transactions are included in net income for the period. . . .

INDUSTRY

OVERVIEW

The number of overweight and obese people worldwide has been increasing due to improving living standards and changing eating patterns, as well as increasingly sedentary lifestyles. The World Health Organization has reported that the world's population is becoming overweight at a rapid pace. According to the organization, in 2000, over one billion people worldwide were overweight and there exists an urgent need to deal with this problem. In the United States, the proportion of U.S. adults who are overweight has increased from 47% to 61% over the last 20 years, and approximately 52 million Americans are currently dieting. . . .

COMPETITION

The weight-loss market includes commercial weight-loss programs, self-help weight-loss products, Internet-based weight-loss products, dietary supplements, weight-loss services administered by doctors, nutritionists and dieticians and weight-loss drugs. Competition among commercial weight-loss programs is largely based on program recognition and reputation and the effectiveness, safety and price of the program. . . .

BUSINESS

OVERVIEW

We are a leading global branded consumer company and the leading provider of weight-loss services in 27 countries around the world. Our programs help people lose weight and maintain their weight loss and, as a result, improve their health, enhance their lifestyles and build self-confidence. At the core of our business are weekly meetings, which promote weight loss through education and group support in conjunction with a flexible, healthy diet. Each week, more than one million members attend approximately 37,000 Weight Watchers meetings, which are run by over 13,000 classroom leaders. Our classroom leaders teach, inspire, motivate and act as role models for our members. . . .

We have experienced strong growth in sales and profits over the last five years since we made the strategic decision to re-focus our meetings exclusively on our group education approach. . . .

The following table sets forth our NACO operations and international attendance for the 1997, 1998, 1999 and 2000 fiscal years and the twelve months ended April 28, 2001. . . .

MARKET OPPORTUNITY

The large and growing global weight-loss market provides us with significant growth potential. In addition, we also believe that we can increase our penetration rate of our target demographic market of overweight women, ages 25 to 64, in our existing major markets as well as in our less developed markets.

The following chart illustrates our level of penetration of our target market . . . [for 13 countries]:

[Table Omitted: eds.]

RELATIVE SIZE OF TARGET MARKET

 . . . We have demonstrated the ability to enter new markets as our program has proven adaptable in 27 countries. We customize our program for each geographic setting by tailoring the program for the local language, culture and food preferences. We believe that our international success proves that our core weight-loss program is effective worldwide and have recently begun operations in Spain and Denmark. . . .

OUR BILLION DOLLAR BRAND

WEIGHT WATCHERS is the leading global weight-loss brand with retail sales of over $1.5 billion in 2000, including licensees and franchisees. Currently, over 97% of U.S. women recognize the WEIGHT WATCHERS brand. In addition, our program is the most widely recommended weight-loss program by U.S. doctors. Our credibility is further enhanced by the endorsement of the U.S. Department of Agriculture. . . .

WEIGHT WATCHERS MEETINGS

We present our program in a series of weekly classes of approximately one hour in duration. Classes are conveniently scheduled throughout the day.

Typically, we hold classes in either meeting rooms rented from civic or religious organizations or in leased locations. [Three pages describing standard operating procedures for classes and core elements of the program's philosophy are omitted. eds.]

ADDITIONAL DELIVERY METHODS

We have developed additional delivery methods for people who, either through circumstance or personal preference, do not attend our classes. For example, we have developed program cookbooks and an AT HOME self-help product that provide information on our diet and guidance on weight loss, as well as CD-ROM versions of our diet for the United Kingdom, Continental Europe and Australia.

Our affiliate and licensee, WeightWatchers.com, recently introduced in the United States WEIGHT WATCHERS ONLINE, an online paid subscription product. . . .

PRODUCT SALES

We sell a range of proprietary products, including snack bars, books, CD-ROMS and POINTS calculators, that is consistent with our brand image. We sell our products primarily through our classroom operations and to our franchisees. In 2000, sales of our proprietary products represented 26% of our revenues, up from 11% in fiscal 1997. . . .

FRANCHISE OPERATIONS

We have enjoyed a mutually beneficial relationship with our franchisees over many years. In our early years, we used an aggressive franchising strategy to quickly establish a meeting infrastructure throughout the world to pre-empt competition. After buying back a significant number of our franchisees, our franchised operations represented approximately 35% of our total worldwide attendance for the nine months ended September 29, 2001. . . . Franchisees typically pay us a fee equal to 10% of their meeting fee revenues.

Our franchisees are responsible for operating classes in their territory using the program we have developed. We provide a central support system for the program and our brand. . . . Most franchise agreements are perpetual and can be terminated only upon a material breach or bankruptcy of the franchisee.

We do not intend to award new franchise territories. From time to time we repurchase franchise territories.

LICENSING

As a highly recognized global brand, WEIGHT WATCHERS is a powerful marketing tool for us and for third parties. We currently license the WEIGHT WATCHERS brand in certain categories of food, apparel, books and other products. . . .

During the period that Heinz owned our company, it developed a number of food product lines under the WEIGHT WATCHERS brand, with hundreds of millions of dollars of retail sales, mostly in the United States and in the United Kingdom.

. . . Heinz has retained a perpetual royalty-free license to continue using our brand in its core food categories. . . .

We have begun focusing on proactively developing new licensing opportunities with a number of food companies and have hired a general manager to focus exclusively on this area. . . .

MARKETING AND PROMOTION

MEMBER REFERRALS

An important source of new members is through word-of-mouth generated by our current and former members. . . .

MEDIA ADVERTISING

. . . We allocate our media advertising on a market-by-market basis, as well as by media vehicle (television, radio, magazines and newspapers), taking into account the target market and the effectiveness of the medium.

DIRECT MAIL

Direct mail is a critical element of our marketing because it targets potential returning members. We maintain a database of current and former members, which we use to focus our direct mailings. During 2000 our NACO operations sent over eight million pieces of direct mail. Most of these mailings are timed to coincide with the start of the diet seasons. . . .

PRICING STRUCTURE AND PROMOTIONS

Our most popular payment structure is a "pay-as-you-go" arrangement. Typically, a new member pays an initial registration fee and then a weekly fee for each class attended, although free registration is often offered as a promotion. Our LIBERTY/LOYALTY payment plan provides members with the option of committing to consecutive weekly attendance with a lower weekly fee with penalties for missed classes or paying a higher weekly fee without the missed meeting penalties. We also offer discounted prepayment options.

PUBLIC RELATIONS AND CELEBRITY ENDORSEMENTS

The focus of our public relations efforts is through our current and former members who have successfully lost weight on our program. . . .

For many years we have also used celebrities to promote and endorse the program. . . .

WEIGHT WATCHERS MAGAZINE

WEIGHT WATCHERS MAGAZINE is an important branded marketing channel that is experiencing strong growth. We re-acquired the rights to publish the magazine in February 2000. Since its U.S. re-launch in March 2000, circulation has grown from zero to over 500,000 in September 2001, and the magazine has a readership of over two million. . . .

WEIGHTWATCHERS.COM

Our affiliate and licensee, WeightWatchers.com, operates the WEIGHT WATCHERS website, which is an important global promotional channel for our brand and businesses. The website contributes value to our classroom business by promoting our brand, advertising Weight Watchers classes and keeping members involved with the program outside the classroom through useful offerings, such as a meeting locator, low calorie recipes, weight-loss news articles, success stories and on-line forums. . . .

Under our agreement with WeightWatchers.com, we granted it an exclusive license to use our trademarks, copyrights and domain names on the Internet in connection with its online weight-loss business. The license agreement provides us with control of how our intellectual property is used. In particular, we have the right to approve WeightWatchers.com's e-commerce activities, strategies and operational plans, marketing programs, privacy policy and materials publicly displayed on the Internet.

We own 19.8% of WeightWatchers.com, or 38.1% on a fully diluted basis (including the exercise of all options and all warrants), and beginning in January 2002, we will receive royalties of 10% of WeightWatchers.com's net revenues.

ENTREPRENEURIAL MANAGEMENT

We run our company in a decentralized and entrepreneurial manner that allows us to develop and test new ideas on a local basis and then implement the most successful ideas across our network. . . .

HISTORY

EARLY DEVELOPMENT

In 1961, Jean Nidetch, the founder of our company, attended a New York City obesity clinic and took what she learned from her personal experience at the obesity clinic and began weight-loss meetings with a group of her overweight friends in the basement of a New York apartment building. Under Ms. Nidetch's leadership, the group members supported each other in their weight-loss efforts, and word of the group's success quickly spread. Ms. Nidetch and Al and Felice Lippert, who all successfully lost weight through these efforts, formally launched Weight Watchers.

HEINZ OWNERSHIP

Recognizing the power of the WEIGHT WATCHERS brand, Heinz acquired us in 1978 in large part to acquire the rights to our name for its food business. . . .

ARTAL OWNERSHIP

In September 1999, Artal Luxembourg acquired us from Heinz. . . .

REGULATION AND LITIGATION

A number of laws and regulations govern our advertising, franchise operations and relations with consumers. . . .

During the mid-1990s, the FTC filed complaints against a number of commercial weight-loss providers alleging violations of the Federal Trade Commission Act by the use and content of advertisements for weight-loss programs that featured testimonials, claims for program success and safety and statements as to program costs to participants. In 1997, we entered into a consent order with the FTC settling all contested issues raised in the complaint filed against us. The consent order requires us to comply with certain procedures and disclosures in connection with our advertisements . . . [and] does not contain any admission of guilt nor require us to pay any civil penalties or damages. . . .

We are involved in legal proceedings incidental to our business. Although the outcome of these matters cannot be predicted with certainty, our management believes that none of these matters will have an adverse effect on our financial condition, results of operations or cash flows.

EMPLOYEES AND SERVICE PROVIDERS

As of September 29, 2001, we had approximately 34,000 employees and service providers, of which 13,100 were located in the United States, 13,000 were located in the United Kingdom, 3,300 were located in Continental Europe and 4,600 were located in Australia and New Zealand. . . . None of our service providers or employees is represented by a labor union. We consider our employee relations to be satisfactory.

PROPERTIES

We are headquartered in Woodbury, New York in a leased office. Each of the four NACO regions has a small regional office. The Woodbury, New York lease expires in 2005, the Paramus, New Jersey lease expires in 2007, and the New York, New York WEIGHT WATCHERS MAGAZINE lease expires in 2002. Our other North American office leases are short-term. Our operations in each country also each have one head office.

We typically hold our classes in third-party locations (typically meeting rooms in well-located civic or religious organizations or space leased in shopping centers). . . .

MANAGEMENT

DIRECTORS AND EXECUTIVE OFFICERS

Set forth below are the names, ages as of June 30, 2001 and current positions with us and our subsidiaries of our executive officers and directors.

NAME	AGE	POSITION
Linda Huett	56	President and Chief Executive Officer, Director
Richard McSorley	57	Chief Operating Officer, NACO
Clive Brothers	47	Chief Operating Officer, Europe
Scott R. Penn	30	Vice President, Australasia
Thomas S. Kiritsis	57	Vice President, Chief Financial Officer
Robert W. Hollweg	58	Vice President, General Counsel and Secretary
Raymond Debbane[1][2]	46	Chairman of the Board
Jonas M. Fajgenbaum	29	Director
Sacha Lainovic[1]	44	Director
Christopher J. Sobecki[2]	43	Director

[1]Member of our compensation and benefits committee.

[2]Member of our audit committee.

[Individual Biographies Omitted: eds.]

BOARD OF DIRECTORS

Our board of directors is currently comprised of five directors. We expect our board of directors to consist of nine members within twelve months of this offering. We expect to add two independent members to our board of directors within three months after the consummation of this offering and a third independent member to our board of directors within twlve months after the consummation of this offering.

BOARD OF DIRECTORS REPORT ON EXECUTIVE COMPENSATION PROGRAMS

Our board of directors oversees the compensation programs of our company, with particular attention to the compensation for our Chief Executive Officer and the other executive officers. It is the responsibility of our board of directors to review, recommend and approve changes to our compensation policies and benefits programs, to administer our stock plans, including approving stock option grants to executive officers and other stock option grants, and to otherwise ensure that our compensation philosophy is consistent with the best interests of our company and is properly implemented.

Our compensation philosophy is to (a) provide a competitive total compensation package that enables us to attract and retain key executive and employee talent needed to accomplish our goals and (b) directly link compensation to improvements in our company's financial and operational performance.

Total compensation is comprised of a base salary plus both cash and non-cash incentive compensation, and is based on our financial performance and other factors, and is delivered through a combination of cash and equity-based awards. . . .

Our board of directors believes that granting stock options provides officers with a strong economic interest in maximizing shareholder returns over the longer term. . . .

Our board of directors will continue to monitor our compensation program in order to maintain the proper balance between cash compensation and equity-based incentives and may consider further revisions in the future, although it is expected that equity-based compensation will remain one of the principal components of compensation.

COMMITTEES OF OUR BOARD OF DIRECTORS

The standing committees of our board of directors will consist of an audit committee and a compensation and benefits committee.

AUDIT COMMITTEE

The principal duties of our audit committee are as follows:

— to oversee that our management has maintained the reliability and integrity of our accounting policies and financial reporting and our disclosure practices;

— to oversee that our management has established and maintained processes to assure that an adequate system of internal control is functioning;

— to oversee that our management has established and maintained processes to assure our compliance with all applicable laws, regulations and corporate policy;

— to review our annual and quarterly financial statements prior to their filing or prior to the release of earnings; and

— to review the performance of the independent accountants and make recommendations to the board of directors regarding the appointment or termination of the independent accountants.

The audit committee has the power to investigate any matter brought to its attention within the scope of its duties and to retain counsel for this purpose where appropriate.

We plan to appoint two independent members of the audit committee within three months following this offering and the third independent member within twelve months after the consummation of this offering.

COMPENSATION AND BENEFITS COMMITTEE

The principal duties of the compensation and benefits committee are as follows:

— to review key employee compensation policies, plans and programs;

— to monitor performance and compensation of our employee-director, officers and other key employees;

— to prepare recommendations and periodic reports to the board of directors concerning these matters; and

— to function as the committee which administers the incentive programs referred to in "Executive Compensation" below. . . .

CLASSES AND TERMS OF DIRECTORS

Our board of directors is divided into three classes, as nearly equal in number as possible, with each director serving a three-year term and one class being elected at each year's annual meeting of shareholders. As of the date of this prospectus, the following individuals are directors and will serve for the terms indicated:

Class 1 Directors (term expiring in 2002)

    Raymond Debbane

    Jonas M. Fajgenbaum

Class 2 Directors (term expiring in 2003)

    Sacha Lainovic

    Christopher J. Sobecki

Class 3 Director (term expiring in 2004)

    Linda Huett

EXECUTIVE COMPENSATION

The following table sets forth for the twelve months ended December 30, 2000, and for the fiscal years ended April 29, 2000 and April 24, 1999, the compensation paid to our President and Chief Executive Officer and to each of the next four most highly compensated executive officers whose total annual salary and bonus was in excess of $100,000.

SUMMARY COMPENSATION TABLE

[Table's Data Omitted: eds.]

In December 1999, our board of directors adopted the "1999 Stock Purchase and Option Plan of Weight Watchers International, Inc. and Subsidiaries" under which selected employees were afforded the opportunity to purchase shares of our common stock and/or were granted options to purchase shares of our common stock. The number of shares available for grant under this plan is 7,058,040 shares of our authorized common stock. The following table sets forth information regarding options granted during the twelve months ended December 30, 2000 to the named executive officers under our stock purchase and option plan.

WEIGHT WATCHERS INTERNATIONAL, INC. AND SUBSIDIARIES OPTION GRANTS FOR THE TWELVE MONTHS ENDED DECEMBER 30, 2000

	INDIVIDUAL GRANTS				
NAME	NUMBER OF SECURITIES UNDERLYING OPTIONS GRANTED	PERCENT OF TOTAL OPTIONS GRANTED TO EMPLOYEES IN TWELVE MONTHS ENDED DECEMBER 30, 2000	EXERCISE OR BASE PRICE (PER SHARE)	EXPIRATION DATE	GRANT DATE PRESENT VALUE[3]
Linda Huett	141,161	28.6%	$2.13	July 4, 2010	$138,600
Thomas S. Kiritsis ...	282,322	57.1%	$2.13	June 14, 2010	$279,000

[3] The estimated grant date's present value is determined using the Black-Scholes model. The adjustments and assumptions incorporated in the Black-Scholes model in estimating the value of the grants include the following: (a) the exercise price of the options equals the fair market value of the underlying stock on the date of grant; (b) an option term of 10 years; (c) dividend yield and volatility of 0%; and (d) a risk free interest rate ranging from 6.20% to 6.26%. The ultimate value, if any, an optionee will realize upon exercise of an option will depend on the excess of the market value of our common stock over the exercise price of the option.

Under our 1999 Stock Purchase and Option Plan, we have the ability to grant stock options, restricted stock, stock appreciation rights and other stock-based awards. Generally, stock options granted under this plan vest and become exercisable in annual increments over five years with respect to one-third of options granted, and the remaining two-thirds of the options vest on the ninth anniversary of the date the options were granted, subject to accelerated vesting upon our achievement of certain performance targets. In any event, the options that vest over five years automatically become fully vested upon the occurrence of a change in control of our company.

[Various Tables Regarding Options and Stock Appreciation Rights Outstanding Omitted: eds.]

RELATED PARTY TRANSACTIONS

THE SUMMARIES OF THE AGREEMENTS DESCRIBED BELOW ARE NOT COMPLETE. YOU SHOULDREAD THE AGREEMENTS IN THEIR ENTIRETY, WHICH HAVE BEEN FILED WITH THE SEC

AS EXHIBITS TO THE REGISTRATION STATEMENT OF WHICH THIS PROSPECTUS IS A PART.

SHAREHOLDERS' AGREEMENTS

Simultaneously with the closing of our acquisition by Artal Luxembourg, we entered into a shareholders' agreement with Artal Luxembourg and Heinz that governs our relationship surrounding our common stock. Subsequent transferees of Artal Luxembourg and Heinz must, subject to limited exceptions, agree to be bound by the terms and provisions of the agreement. Heinz has sold all shares of our common stock held by it and accordingly no longer has any rights or obligations under this agreement. We and Artal Luxembourg recently terminated this agreement.

Shortly after our acquisition by Artal Luxembourg, we entered into a shareholders' agreement with Artal Luxembourg and Merchant Capital, Inc., Richard and Heather Penn, Longisland International Limited, Envoy Partners and Scotiabanc, Inc. that governs our relationship surrounding our common stock held by these parties other than Artal Luxembourg. Without the consent of Artal Luxembourg, transfers of our common stock by these shareholders are restricted with certain exceptions. . . .

REGISTRATION RIGHTS AGREEMENT

Simultaneously with the closing of our acquisition by Artal Luxembourg, we entered into a registration rights agreement with Artal Luxembourg and Heinz. The registration rights agreement grants Artal Luxem-bourg the right to require us to register its shares of our common stock for public sale under the Securities Act (1) upon demand and (2) in the event that we conduct certain types of registered offerings. . . .

PREFERRED SHAREHOLDERS' AGREEMENT

Simultaneously with the closing of our acquisition by Artal Luxembourg, we entered into a preferred shareholders' agreement with Heinz that governs our relationship concerning our Series A Preferred Stock. Subsequent transferees of Heinz, subject to limited exceptions, must agree to be bound by the terms and provisions of this agreement. Artal Luxembourg and we have a preemptive right to acquire the preferred stock from Heinz if Heinz receives an offer to purchase any or all of its preferred stock from a third party and it wishes to accept the offer. As a result of this offering, Heinz has the right to require us to redeem limited by the provisions contained in our credit agreement and the indentures pursuant to which our senior subordinated notes were issued. . . .

LIMITED LIABILITY COMPANY AGREEMENT

Simultaneously with the closing of our acquisition by Artal Luxembourg, we contributed $2,500 in exchange for a 50% membership interest in

WW Foods, LLC, a Delaware limited liability company. Heinz owns the remaining 50% interest. The purpose of WW Foods is to own, maintain and preserve WEIGHT WATCHERS food and beverage trademarks that were contributed to it by Heinz. WW Foods serves as the vehicle for licensing rights in those food and beverage trademarks to us and to Heinz, and for the licensing of program information by our company to Heinz.

LICENSING AGREEMENTS

The licensing agreements govern the ownership and rights to use the WEIGHT WATCHERS and other trademarks, service marks and related rights among our company, Heinz and WW Foods. As described below, the licensing agreements address the parties' respective ownership and rights to use food and beverage trademarks, service marks, program standards, program information, program information trademarks and third party licenses. Heinz is also a party to the operating agreement, which helps preserve and enhance these trademarks, service marks and related rights and facilitates their orderly use by each party.

FOOD AND BEVERAGE TRADEMARKS

Under the licensing agreements, we distributed to Heinz and Heinz contributed to WW Foods all WEIGHT WATCHERS trademarks and other trademarks we owned relating to food and beverage products. However, Heinz retained certain trademarks previously used by Heinz in connection with those food and beverage trademarks that do not include the WEIGHT WATCHERS name (including, for example, SMART ONES), which we distributed to Heinz. At the closing of our acquisition by Artal Luxembourg, WW Foods granted an exclusive, worldwide, royalty-free, perpetual license to use the food and beverage trademarks:

— to Heinz, for worldwide use on food products in specified product categories . . . ; and
— to us, for use on all other food and beverage products. . . .

At the closing of our acquisition by Artal Luxembourg, we granted to Heinz an exclusive, worldwide, royalty-free license to use those food and beverage trademarks (or any portion covering food and beverage products) that we hold in custody for the benefit of WW Foods in connection with the other products licensed to Heinz by WW Foods. . . .

PROGRAM STANDARDS

We have exclusive control of the dietary principles to be followed in any eating or lifestyle regimen to facilitate weight loss or weight control employed by the classroom business such as WINNING POINTS. Except for specified limitations concerning products currently sold and extensions of existing product lines, Heinz may use the food and beverage related trademarks only on Heinz licensed products that have been specially formulated to be compatible with our dietary principles. We have exclusive responsibility for enforcing compliance with our dietary principles. . . .

THIRD PARTY LICENSES

Under the licensing agreements, we assigned to Heinz all licenses that we previously granted to third parties, and Heinz retained all existing sub-licenses granted by it to third parties under a license previously granted to Heinz, that relate to the manufacture, distribution or sale of food and beverage products.

MANAGEMENT AGREEMENT

Simultaneously with the closing of our acquisition by Artal Luxembourg, we entered into a management agreement with The Invus Group, Ltd., the independent investment advisor to Artal Luxembourg. Under this agreement, The Invus Group provides us with management, consulting and other services in exchange for an annual fee equal to the greater of one million dollars or one percent of our EBITDA (as defined in the indentures relating to our senior subordinated notes), plus any related out-of-pocket expenses. This agreement is terminable at the option of The Invus Group at any time or by us at any time after Artal Luxembourg owns less than a majority of our voting stock.

CORPORATE AGREEMENTM

We have entered into a corporate agreement with Artal Luxembourg. We have agreed that, so long as Artal Luxembourg beneficially owns 10% or more, but less than a majority of our then outstanding voting stock, Artal Luxembourg will have the right to nominate a number of directors approximately equal to that percentage multiplied by the number of directors on our board. This right to nominate directors will not restrict Artal Luxembourg from nominating a greater number of directors.

We have agreed with Artal Luxembourg that both Weight Watchers and Artal Luxembourg have the right to:

— engage in the same or similar business activities as the other party;

— do business with any customer or client of the other party; and

— employ or engage any officer or employee of the other party.

Neither Artal Luxembourg nor we, nor our respective related parties, will be liable to each other as a result of engaging in any of these activities.

Under the corporate agreement, if one of our officers or directors who also serves as an officer, director or advisor of Artal Luxembourg becomes aware of a potential transaction related primarily to the group education-based weight-loss business that may represent a corporate opportunity for both Artal Luxembourg and us, the officer, director or advisor has no duty to present that opportunity to Artal Luxembourg, and we will have the sole right to pursue the transaction if our board so determines. If one of our officers or directors who also serves as an officer, director or advisor of Artal Luxembourg becomes aware of any other potential transaction that may represent a corporate opportunity for both Artal Luxembourg and us, the officer or director will have a duty to present that opportunity to Artal Luxembourg, and Artal Luxembourg will have the sole right to pursue the transaction if Artal Luxembourg's board so determines. If one of our officers or directors who does not serve as an officer, director or advisor of Artal Luxembourg becomes aware of a potential transaction that may represent a corporate opportunity for both Artal Luxembourg and us, neither the officer nor the director nor we have a duty to present that opportunity to Artal Luxembourg, and we may pursue the transaction if our board so determines. . . .

WEIGHTWATCHERS.COM NOTE

On September 10, 2001, we amended and restated our loan agreement with WeightWatchers.com, increasing the aggregate commitment thereunder to $34.5 million. The principal amount may be advanced at any time or from time to time prior to July 31, 2003. The note bears interest at 13% per year, beginning on January 1, 2002, which interest, except as set forth below, shall be paid semi-annually starting on March 31, 2002. All principal outstanding under this note will be payable in six semi-annual installments, starting on March 31, 2004. . . .

WEIGHTWATCHERS.COM WARRANT AGREEMENTS

Under the warrant agreements that we entered with WeightWatchers. com, we have received warrants to purchase an additional 6,394,997 shares of WeightWatchers.com's common stock in connection with the loans that we made to WeightWatchers.com under the note described above. These warrants will expire from November 24, 2009 to September 10, 2011 and may be exercised at a price of $7.14 per share of Weight-Watchers.com's common stock until their expiration. We own 19.8% of the outstanding common stock of WeightWatchers.com, or 38.1% on a fully diluted basis (including the exercise of all options and all the warrants we own in WeightWatchers.com).

COLLATERAL ASSIGNMENT AND SECURITY AGREEMENT

In connection with the WeightWatchers.com note, we entered into a collateral assignment and security agreement whereby we obtained a security interest in the assets of WeightWatchers.com. Our security interest in those assets will terminate when the note has been paid in full.

WEIGHTWATCHERS.COM INTELLECTUAL PROPERTY LICENSE

We have entered into an amended and restated intellectual property license agreement with WeightWatchers.com that governs WeightWatchers.com's right to use our trademarks and materials related to the Weight Watchers program. . . .

Beginning in January 2002, WeightWatchers.com will pay us a royalty of 10% of the net revenues it earns through its online activities.

We retain exclusive ownership of all of the trademarks and materials that we license to WeightWatchers.com and of the derivative works created by WeightWatchers.com. . . .

The license agreement provides us with control over the use of our intellectual property. We will have the right to approve any e-commerce activities, any materials, sublicense, communication to consumers, products, privacy policy, strategies, marketing and operational plans Weight-Watchers.com intends to use or implement in connection with its online weight-loss business. . . .

WEIGHTWATCHERS.COM REGISTRATION RIGHTS AGREEMENT

We entered into a registration rights agreement with WeightWatchers.com, Artal Luxembourg and Heinz with respect to our shares in WeightWatchers.com. Heinz has resold all of its shares in WeightWatchers.com back to WeightWatchers.com and thus no longer has any rights under this agreement. The registration rights agreement grants Artal Luxembourg the right to require WeightWatchers.com to register its shares of Weight-Watchers.com common stock upon demand and also grants us and Artal Luxembourg rights to register and sell shares of WeightWatchers.com's common stock in the event it conducts certain types of registered offerings.

WEIGHTWATCHERS.COM LEASE GUARANTEE

We have guaranteed the performance of WeightWatcher.com's lease of its office space at 888 Seventh Avenue, New York, New York. The annual rental rate is $459,000 plus increases for operating expenses and real estate taxes. The lease expires in September 2003.

NELLSON CO-PACK AGREEMENT

We entered into an agreement with Nellson Nutraceutical, a subsidiary of Artal Luxembourg, to purchase snack bar and powder products manufactured by Nellson Nutraceutical for sale at our meetings. . . . We purchased $4.9 million and $4.3 million, respectively, of products from Nellson Nutraceutical during the eight months ended December 30, 2000 and the twelve months ended April 29, 2000. The term of the agreement runs through December 31, 2004, and we have the option to renew the agreement for successive one-year periods by providing written notice to Nellson Nutraceutical.

PRINCIPAL AND SELLING SHAREHOLDERS

The following table sets forth information regarding the beneficial ownership of our common stock by (1) all persons known by us to own beneficially more than 5% of our common stock, (2) our chief executive officer and each of the named executive officers, (3) each director, (4) all directors and executive officers as a group and (5) each selling shareholder.

Beneficial ownership is determined in accordance with the rules of the Securities and Exchange Commission. . . .

Our capital stock consists of our common stock and our preferred stock. As of September 29, 2001, there were 105,407,142 shares of our common stock and 1,000,000 shares of our preferred stock outstanding.

NAME OF BENEFICIAL OWNER	AS OF SEPTEMBER 29, 2001		SHARES TO BE SOLD IN OFFERING	IMMEDIATELY AFTER THIS OFFERING	
	SHARES	PERCENT		SHARES	PERCENT
Artal Luxembourg S.A	99,109,939	94.0%	16,047,516	83,062,423	78.8%
Linda Huett	199,979	*	—	199,978	*
Richard McSorley	94,108	*	—	94,108	*
Clive Brothers	164,688	*	—	164,688	*
Scott R. Penn	299,968	*	—	299,967	*
Thomas S. Kiritsis	164,689	*	—	164,688	*
Robert W. Hollweg	188,215	*	—	188,215	*
Raymond Debbane	—	—	—	—	—
Sacha Lainovic	—	—	—	—	—
Christopher J. Sobecki	—	—	—	—	—
Jonas M. Fajgenbaum	—	—	—	—	—
All directors and executive officers as a group (10 people)	1,111,644	1.1%	—	1,111,644	1.1%
Richard and Heather Penn	1,246,921	1.2%	941,072	305,849	*
Merchant Capital, Inc.	941,072	*	152,375	788,697	*
Scotiabanc, Inc.	941,072	*	152,375	788,697	*
Longisland International Limited	658,751	*	106,662	552,089	*

*Less than 1.0%.

[Notes to Schedule Omitted: eds.]

In addition, certain of the selling shareholders have granted the underwriters the right to purchase up to an additional 2,610,000 shares of common stock to cover over-allotments. If the underwriters exercise this over-allotment option in full, Artal Luxembourg will beneficially own 76.4% of our common stock after this offering.

DESCRIPTION OF INDEBTEDNESS

The following are summaries of the material terms and conditions of our principal indebtedness.

SENIOR CREDIT FACILITIES

. . .

SENIOR SUBORDINATED NOTES

. . .

DESCRIPTION OF CAPITAL STOCK

Our authorized capital stock consists of (1) 1.0 billion shares of common stock, no par value, of which 105,407,142 million shares are issued and outstanding and (2) 250,000,000 shares of preferred stock, no par value, of which 1,000,000 shares are issued and outstanding. As of September 29, 2001, there were 52 holders of our common stock. . . .

The following summary describes elements of our articles of incorporation and bylaws after giving effect to the offering.

COMMON STOCK

VOTING RIGHTS. The holders of our common stock are entitled to one vote per share on all matters submitted for action by the shareholders. There is no provision for cumulative voting with respect to the election of directors. Accordingly, a holder of more than 50% of the shares of our common stock can, if it so chooses, elect all of our directors. In that event, the holders of the remaining shares will not be able to elect any directors.

DIVIDEND RIGHTS. All shares of our common stock are entitled to share equally in any dividends our board of directors may declare from legally available sources. Our senior credit facilities and indentures impose restrictions on our ability to declare dividends with respect to our common stock.

LIQUIDATION RIGHTS. Upon liquidation or dissolution of our company, whether voluntary or involuntary, all shares of our common stock are entitled to share equally in the assets available for distribution to shareholders after payment of all of our prior obligations, including our preferred stock.

OTHER MATTERS. The holders of our common stock have no preemptive or conversion rights and our common stock is not subject to further calls or assessments by us. There are no redemption or sinking fund provisions applicable to the common stock. All outstanding shares of our common stock, including the common stock offered in this offering, are fully paid and non-assessable.

PREFERRED STOCK

We have one million shares of Series A Preferred Stock issued and out-standing. Holders of our Series A Preferred Stock are entitled to receive dividends at an annual rate of 6% payable annually in arrears. The liqui-dation preference of our Series A Preferred Stock is $25 per share. In the event of a liquidation, dissolution or winding up of our company, the holders of shares of our Series A Preferred Stock will be entitled to be paid out of our assets available for distribution to our shareholders an amount in cash equal to the $25 liquidation preference per share plus all accrued and unpaid dividends prior to the distribution of any assets to holders of shares of our common stock.

Except as required by law, the holders of our preferred stock have no voting rights with respect to their shares of preferred stock other than that the approval of holders of a majority of the outstanding shares of our preferred stock, voting as a class, will be required to amend, repeal or change any of the provisions of our articles of incorporation in any manner that would alter or change the powers, preferences or special rights of our preferred stock in a way that would affect them adversely. Without the consent of each holder of the Series A Preferred Stock, no amendment may reduce the dividend payable on or the liquidation value of the Series A Preferred Stock.

We may redeem the Series A Preferred Stock, in whole or in part, at any time or from time to time, at our option, at a price per share equal to 100% of the liquidation value of the preferred stock plus all accrued and unpaid dividends. . . .

Our board of directors also has the authority, without any further vote or action by the shareholders, to designate and issue preferred stock in one or more additional series and to designate the rights, preferences and privileges of each series, which may be greater than the rights of the common stock. It is not possible to state the actual effect of the issuance of any additional series of preferred stock upon the rights of holders of the common stock until the board of directors determines the specific rights of the holders of that series. However, the effects might include, among other things:

— restricting dividends on the common stock;
— diluting the voting power of the common stock;
— impairing the liquidation rights of the common stock; or
— delaying or preventing a change in control without further action by the shareholders.

OPTIONS

As of September 29, 2001, there were outstanding 5,763,692 shares of our common stock issuable upon exercise of outstanding stock options and

1,294,348 shares of our common stock reserved for future issuance under our existing stock option plan.

AUTHORIZED BUT UNISSUED CAPITAL STOCK

The listing requirements of the New York Stock Exchange, which would apply so long as the common stock remains listed on the New York Stock Exchange, require shareholder approval of certain issuances equal to or exceeding 20% of then-outstanding voting power or then-outstanding number of shares of common stock. These additional shares may be used for a variety of corporate purposes, including future public offerings, to raise additional capital or to facilitate acquisitions.

One of the effects of the existence of unissued and unreserved common stock or preferred stock may be to enable our board of directors to issue shares to persons friendly to current management, which issuance could render more difficult or discourage an attempt to obtain control of our company by means of a merger, tender offer, proxy contest or otherwise, and thereby protect the continuity of our management and possibly deprive the shareholders of opportunities to sell their shares of common stock at prices higher than prevailing market prices.

CERTAIN PROVISIONS OF VIRGINIA LAW AND OUR CHARTER AND BYLAWS

Some provisions of Virginia law and our articles of incorporation and bylaws could make the following more difficult:

— acquisition of us by means of a tender offer;
— acquisition of us by means of a proxy contest or otherwise; or
— removal of our incumbent officers and directors.

These provisions, summarized below, are intended to discourage coercive takeover practices and inadequate takeover bids. These provisions are also designed to encourage persons seeking to acquire control of us to first negotiate with our board. We believe that the benefits of increased protection give us the potential ability to negotiate with the proponent of an unfriendly or unsolicited proposal to acquire or restructure us and outweigh the disadvantages of discouraging these proposals because negotiation of these proposals could result in an improvement of their terms.

ELECTION AND REMOVAL OF DIRECTORS

Our board of directors is divided into three classes. . . . This system of electing and removing directors may discourage a third party from making a tender offer or otherwise attempting to obtain control of us because it generally makes it more difficult for shareholders to replace a majority of our directors.

Our articles of incorporation and bylaws do not provide for cumulative voting in the election of directors.

BOARD MEETINGS

Our bylaws provide that the chairman of the board or any two of our directors may call special meetings of the board of directors.

SHAREHOLDER MEETINGS

Our articles of incorporation provide that special meetings of shareholders may be called by the chairman of our board of directors or our president or by a resolution adopted by our board of directors. In addition, our articles of incorporation provide that Artal Luxembourg and certain of its transferees have the right to call special meetings of shareholders prior to the date it ceases to beneficially own 20% of our then-outstanding common stock.

REQUIREMENTS FOR ADVANCE NOTIFICATION OF SHAREHOLDER NOMINATIONS AND PROPOSALS

Our bylaws establish advance notice procedures with respect to shareholder proposals and the nomination of candidates for election as directors, other than nominations made by or at the direction of our board of directors or a committee of the board of directors or by Artal Luxembourg and certain of its transferees when nominating its director designees. In addition, our bylaws provide that so long as Artal Luxembourg or certain of its transferees beneficially owns a majority of our then-outstanding common stock, the foregoing advance notice procedures for shareholder proposals will not apply to it.

SHAREHOLDER ACTION BY WRITTEN CONSENT

Virginia law generally requires shareholder action to be taken only at a meeting of shareholders and permits shareholders to act only by written consent with the unanimous written consent of all shareholders.

AMENDMENT OF ARTICLES OF INCORPORATION AND BYLAW PROVISIONS

Amendment of the provisions described above in our articles of incorporation generally will require an affirmative vote of our directors, as well as the affirmative vote of at least 80% of our then-outstanding voting stock, except that at any time that Artal Luxembourg or certain of its transferees beneficially owns a majority of our then-outstanding common stock, the anti-takeover provisions of our articles of incorporation may be amended by the affirmative vote of a majority of our then-outstanding voting stock. . . .

RIGHTS AGREEMENT

We intend to adopt, prior to consummation of this offering, a rights agreement, subject to the approval of our board. Under the rights agreement, one right will be issued and attached to each share of our common stock including eleven shares that are outstanding. Each right will entitle the holder, in the circumstances described below, to purchase from our company a unit consisting of one one-hundredth of a share of Series B junior participating preferred stock, no par value per share, at an exercise price of $____ per right, subject to adjustment in certain events. [Five-page description of Rights Provision omitted: eds.]

LIABILITY OF OFFICERS AND DIRECTORS

Our articles of incorporation require us to indemnify any director, officer or employee who was or is a party to any claim, action or proceeding by reason of his being or having been a director, officer or employee of our company or any other corporation, entity or plan while serving at our request, unless he or she engaged in willful misconduct or a knowing violation of law. Insofar as indemnification for liabilities arising under the Securities Act of 1933 may be permitted to directors, officers or persons controlling us pursuant to the foregoing provisions, we have been informed that, in the opinion of the SEC, indemnification for liabilities under the Securities Act is against public policy and is unenforceable.

ANTI-TAKEOVER STATUTES

We have opted out of the Virginia anti-takeover law regulating "control share acquisitions." . . .

REGISTRAR AND TRANSFER AGENT

The registrar and transfer agent for the common stock is EquiServe Trust Company, N.A.

LISTING

Our common stock has been authorized for listing on the New York Stock Exchange under the symbol "WTW."

SHARES ELIGIBLE FOR FUTURE SALE

Prior to this offering, there has not been any public market for our common stock, and we cannot predict what effect, if any, market sales of shares of common stock or the availability of shares of common stock for sale will have on the market price of our common stock. Nevertheless, sales of substantial amounts of common stock, including shares issued upon the exercise of outstanding options, in the public market, or the perception that these sales could occur, could materially and adversely affect the market price of our common stock and could impair our future ability to raise capital through the sale of our equity or equity-related securities at a time and price that we deem appropriate.

Upon the closing of this offering, we will have outstanding an aggregate of 105,407,142 shares of common stock. Of the outstanding shares, the shares sold in this offering will be freely tradable without restriction or further registration under the Securities Act, except that any shares held by our "affiliates," as that term is defined under Rule 144 of the Securities Act, may be sold only in compliance with the limitations described below. The remaining shares of common stock will be deemed "restricted securities" as defined under Rule 144. Restricted securities may be sold in the public market only if registered or if they qualify for an exemption from registration under Rule 144 or 144(k) under the Securities Act, which we summarize below.

Subject to the lock-up agreements described below, the employee shareholders agreements and the provisions of Rules 144 and 144(k), additional shares of our common stock will be available for sale in the public market under exemptions from registration requirements as follows:

NUMBER OF SHARES	DATE
87,889,507	After 180 days from the date of this prospectus
117,635	At various times after 180 days from the date of this prospectus

Artal Luxembourg, which will own 78.8% of our shares (or 76.4% if the underwriters exercise their over-allotment option in full) upon the closing of this offering, has the ability to cause us to register the resale of its shares.

RULE 144

[Summary of Rule 144 Omitted: eds.]

LOCK-UP AGREEMENTS

We have agreed that we will not offer, sell, contract to sell, pledge or otherwise dispose of, directly or indirectly, or file with the SEC a registration statement under the Securities Act relating to, any shares of our common stock or securities convertible into or exchangeable or exercisable for any shares of our common stock, or publicly disclose the intention to make any offer, sale, pledge, disposition or filing, without the prior written consent of Credit Suisse First Boston Corporation for a period of 180 days after the date of this prospectus. . . .

Our executive officers and directors and the selling shareholders have [also agreed to a lockup]. . . .

Following this offering, we intend to file a registration statement on Form S-8 under the Securities Act with respect to up to 7,058,040 shares of our common stock that are reserved for issuance pursuant to our stock option plan. . . . However, shares received by employees upon exercise of their options will be subject to certain lock-up agreements. . . .

CERTAIN U.S. FEDERAL INCOME TAX CONSEQUENCES

The following summary describes the material U.S. federal income tax consequences as of the date hereof of the purchase, ownership and disposition of our common stock by a Non-U.S. Holder (as defined below) who holds our common stock as a capital asset. . . . YOU SHOULD CONSULT YOUR OWN TAX ADVISOR CONCERNING THE PARTICULAR U.S. INCOME TAX CONSEQUENCES TO YOU OF THE OWNERSHIP OF THE COMMON STOCK, AS WELL AS THE CONSEQUENCES TO YOU ARISING UNDER THE LAWS OF ANY OTHER TAXING JURISDICTION.

NON-U.S. HOLDERS

. . .

TAXATION OF THE COMMON STOCK

DIVIDENDS. Distributions on our common stock will constitute dividends for United States federal income tax purposes to the extent of our current or accumulated earnings and profits as determined under U.S. federal income tax principles. In general, distributions paid to you will be subject to withholding U.S. federal income tax at a 30% rate or such lower rate as may be specified by an applicable income tax treaty. If you wish to claim the benefit of an applicable treaty rate (and avoid backup withholding as discussed below under "Information Reporting and Backup Withholding"), you will be required to satisfy applicable certification and other requirements. . . .

GAIN ON DISPOSITION OF COMMON STOCK. You generally will not be subject to U.S. federal income tax with respect to gain recognized on a sale or other disposition of common stock unless (i) the gain is effectively connected with your trade or business in the United States, and, where a tax treaty applies, is attributable to a U.S. permanent establishment, (ii) you are an individual and you are present in the United States for 183 or more days in the taxable year of the sale or other disposition and certain other conditions are met, or (iii) you hold (or held at any time within the shorter of the five-year period preceding the sale or other disposition or the period you held our common stock) more than 5% of our common stock and we are or have been at any such time a U.S. real property holding corporation for U.S. federal income tax purposes. . . .

UNDERWRITING

Under the terms and subject to the conditions contained in an underwriting agreement dated   , 2001, the selling shareholders have agreed to sell to the underwriters named below, for whom Credit Suisse First Boston Corporation and Goldman, Sachs & Co. are acting as representatives, the following respective numbers of shares of common stock:

UNDERWRITER	NUMBER OF SHARES
Credit Suisse First Boston Corporation	
Goldman, Sachs & Co.	
Merrill Lynch, Pierce, Fenner & Smith Incorporated	
Salomon Smith Barney Inc.	
UBS Warburg LLC	
Total	17,400,000

The underwriting agreement provides that the underwriters are obligated to purchase all the shares of common stock in the offering if any are purchased, other than those shares covered by the over-allotment option described below. The underwriting agreement also provides that, if an underwriter defaults, the purchase commitments of non-defaulting underwriters may be increased or the offering may be terminated.

Certain of the selling shareholders have granted to the underwriters a 30-day option to purchase on a pro rata basis up to an aggregate of 2,610,000 additional shares at the initial public offering price less the underwriting discounts and commissions. The option may be exercised only to cover any over-allotments of common stock.

The underwriters propose to offer the shares of common stock initially at the public offering price on the cover page of this prospectus and to selling group members at that price less a selling concession of $____ per share. The underwriters and selling group members may allow a discount of $____ per share on sales to other broker/dealers. After the initial public offering the representatives may change the public offering price and concession and discount to broker/dealers.

The following table summarizes the compensation the selling shareholders will pay and the estimated expenses we will pay:

	PER SHARE		TOTAL	
	WITHOUT OVER-ALLOTMENT	WITH OVER-ALLOTMENT	WITHOUT OVER-ALLOTMENT	WITH OVER-ALLOTMENT
Underwriting discounts and commissions paid by selling shareholders... $	$	$	$	$
Expenses payable by us .... $	$	$	$	$

The representatives have informed us that the underwriters do not expect discretionary sales to exceed 5% of the shares of common stock being offered.

We and the selling shareholders have agreed to indemnify the underwriters against liabilities under the Securities Act, or to contribute to payments which the underwriters may be required to make in that respect.

Prior to this offering, there has been no public market for our common stock. The initial public offering price will be determined by negotiation between the selling shareholders and the representatives and will not necessarily reflect the market price of the common stock following the offering. The principal factors that will be considered in determining the public offering price will include:

— the information in this prospectus and otherwise available to the underwriters;

— market conditions for initial public offerings;

— the history and the prospects for the industry in which we compete;

— the ability of our management;

— the prospects for our future earnings;

— the present state of our development and our current financial condition;

— recent market prices of, and the demand for, publicly traded common stock of generally comparable companies; and

— the general condition of the securities markets at the time of this offering.

We offer no assurances that the initial public offering price will correspond to the price at which the common stock will trade in the public market subsequent to the offering or that an active trading market for the common stock will develop and continue after the offering.

Our common stock has been authorized for listing on the New York Stock Exchange under the symbol "WTW."

In connection with the offering, the underwriters may engage in stabilizing transactions, over-allotment transactions, syndicate covering transactions and penalty bids in accordance with Regulation M under the Securities Exchange Act of 1934.

— Stabilizing transactions permit bids to purchase the underlying security so long as the stabilizing bids do not exceed a specified maximum.

— Over-allotment involves sales by the underwriters of shares in excess of the number of shares the underwriters are obligated to purchase, which creates a syndicate short position. . . .

— Penalty bids permit the representatives to reclaim a selling concession from a syndicate member when the common stock originally sold by the syndicate member is purchased in a stabilizing or syndicate covering transaction to cover syndicate short positions.

These stabilizing transactions . . . and penalty bids may have the effect of raising or maintaining the market price of our common stock or preventing or retarding a decline in the market price of the common stock. As a result, the price of our common stock may be higher than the price that might otherwise exist in the open market. . . .

Some of the underwriters and their affiliates have provided, and may provide in the future, investment banking and other financial services for us in the ordinary course of business for which they have received and would receive customary compensation. Credit Suisse First Boston, New York branch, an affiliate of Credit Suisse First Boston Corporation, is an agent and a lender under our senior credit facilities, and Credit Suisse First Boston Corporation was one of the joint book-running managers for, and an initial purchaser of, our 13% senior subordinated notes due 2009. In addition, Credit Suisse First Boston, New York branch, was a joint lead arranger and joint book manager for our $50 million increase to our senior credit facilities.

Credit Suisse First Boston Corporation also served as financial advisor to Artal Luxembourg in its acquisition of us. The decision of Credit Suisse First Boston Corporation to underwrite our common stock offered hereby was made independent of Credit Suisse First Boston, New York branch, which had no involvement in determining whether to underwrite our common stock under this offering or the terms of this offering. . . .

LEGAL MATTERS

The validity of the issuance of the shares of common stock to be sold in the offering will be passed upon for us by our special Virginia counsel, Hunton & Williams, Richmond, Virginia. Certain legal matters in connection with the issuance of the common stock to be sold in the offering will be passed upon for us by Simpson Thacher & Bartlett, New York, New York. The underwriters have been represented by Cravath, Swaine & Moore, New York, New York.

EXPERTS

The financial statements as of December 30, 2000, April 29, 2000 and April 24, 1999 and for each of the fiscal years ended April 29, 2000, April 24, 1999 and April 25, 1998, the eight months ended December 30, 2000 and the year ended December 30, 2000 included in this prospectus have been so included in reliance on the report of PricewaterhouseCoopers LLP, independent accountants, given on the authority of said firm as experts in auditing and accounting.

WHERE YOU CAN FIND ADDITIONAL INFORMATION

We file annual, quarterly and current reports and other information with the SEC. You may access and read our SEC filings, including the complete registration statement and all of the exhibits to it, through the SEC's Internet site at www.sec.gov. . . .

We have filed with the SEC a registration statement under the Securities Act with respect to the common stock offered by this prospectus. This prospectus, which constitutes part of the registration statement, does not contain all of the information presented in the registration statement and its exhibits and schedules. Our descriptions in this prospectus of the provisions of documents filed as exhibits to the registration statement or otherwise filed with the SEC are only summaries of the terms of those documents that we consider material. If you want a complete description of the content of the documents, you should obtain the documents yourself by following the procedures described above.

You may request copies of the filings, at no cost, by telephone at (516) 390-1400 or by mail at: 175 Crossways Park West, Woodbury, New York 11797-2055, Attention: Secretary.

INDEX TO FINANCIAL STATEMENTS

F-1

REPORT OF INDEPENDENT ACCOUNTANTS

To the Board of Directors of Weight Watchers International, Inc.:

In our opinion, the accompanying consolidated balance sheets and the related consolidated statements of operations, of cash flows and of changes in shareholders' deficit, parent company investment and comprehensive income present fairly, in all material respects, the consolidated financial position of Weight WatchersInternational, Inc. and its subsidiaries at December 30, 2000, April 29, 2000 and April 24, 1999, and the results of their operations and their cash flows for the eight months ended December 30, 2000 and for each of the three years in the period ended April 29, 2000, in conformity with accounting principles generally accepted in the United States of America. These financial statements are the responsibility of the Company's management; our responsibility is to express an opinion on these financial statements based on our audits. We conducted our audits of these statements in accordance with auditing standards generally accepted in the United States of America, which require that we plan and perform the audit to obtain reasonable assurance about whether the financial statements are free of material misstatement. An audit includes examining, on a test basis, evidence supporting the amounts and disclosures in the financial statements, assessing the accounting principles used and significant estimates made by management, and evaluating the over-all financial statement presentation. We believe that our audits provide a reasonable basis for our opinion.

PricewaterhouseCoopers LLP

New York, New York

[All Financial Statements Omitted: eds.]

PART II

INFORMATION NOT REQUIRED IN PROSPECTUS

ITEM 13.   OTHER EXPENSES OF ISSUANCE AND DISTRIBUTION.

The actual and estimated expenses in connection with the offering, all of which will be borne by Weight Watchers International, Inc. are as follows:

SEC Registration Fee	$ 115,058
Printing and Engraving Expenses	275,000
Legal Fees	1,000,000
Accounting Fees	500,000
NYSE Listing Fees	250,000
NASD Filing Fee	30,500
Miscellaneous	50,000
Total	$2,220,558

ITEM 14.   INDEMNIFICATION OF DIRECTORS AND OFFICERS.

Our articles of incorporation provide for the indemnification of our directors and officers in a variety of circumstances, which may include in-demnification for liabilities under the Securities Act. . . . Weight Watchers also carries insurance on behalf of its directors, officers, employees or agents that may cover liabilities under the Securities Act. . . .

ITEM 15.   RECENT SALES OF UNREGISTERED SECURITIES.

During the three years preceding the filing of this registration statement, the Registrant sold shares of and issued options for its common stock and preferred stock in the amounts, at the times, and for the aggregate amounts of consideration listed below without registration under the Securities Act of 1933. Exemption from registration under the Securities Act for each of the following sales is claimed under Section 4(2) of the Securities Act because each of the transactions was by the issuer and did not involve a public offering: . . .

ITEM 16.   EXHIBITS AND FINANCIAL STATEMENT SCHEDULES.

EXHIBITS

EXHIBIT NO.	DESCRIPTION OF EXHIBIT
1.1**	Form of Underwriting Agreement.
3.1**	Form of Amended and Restated Articles of Incorporation of Weight Watchers International, Inc.
3.2**	Form of Amended and Restated Bylaws of Weight Watchers International, Inc.
4.1	Senior Subordinated Dollar Notes Indenture. . . .
4.2	Guarantee Agreement. . . .
4.3	Senior Subordinated Euro Notes Indenture. . . .
4.4	Guarantee Agreement. . . .
4.5**	Form of Rights Agreement between Weight Watchers International, Inc. and EquiServe Trust Company, N.A.
4.6**	Specimen of stock certificate representing Weight Watchers International, Inc.'s common stock, no par value.
5.1**	Opinion of Hunton & Williams.
10.1**	Amended and Restated Credit Agreement. . . .
10.2	Preferred Stockholders' Agreement. . . .
10.3	Stockholders' Agreement. . . .
10.4	License Agreement, dated as of September 29, 1999, between WW Foods, LLC and Weight Watchers International, Inc. (Incorporated by reference to Exhibit 10.4 of Weight Watchers International, Inc.'s Form S-4 Registration Statement No. 333-92005).
10.5	License Agreement . . . between Weight Watchers International, Inc. and H.J. Heinz Company
10.6	License Agreement . . . between WW Foods, LLC and H.J. Heinz Company
10.7	LLC Agreement. . . .
10.8	Operating Agreement . . . between Weight Watchers International, Inc. and H.J. Heinz Company (Incorporated by reference to Exhibit 10.8 of Weight Watchers International, Inc.'s Form S-4 Registration Statement No. 333-92005).
10.9**	Stockholders' Agreement . . . among Weight Watchers International, Inc., Artal Luxembourg S.A., Merchant Capital, Inc., Logo Incorporated Pty. Ltd., Longisland International Limited, Envoy Partners and Scotiabanc, Inc. Registration Rights Agreement . . . among WeightWatchers.com, Inc., Weight Watchers International, Inc., H.J. Heinz Company and Artal Luxembourg S.A. . . . Stockholders' Agreement . . . among WeightWatchers.com, Weight Watchers International, Inc., Artal Luxembourg S.A. and H.J. Heinz Company. . . .
10.12	Letter Agreement. . . .

10.13	Agreement of Lease. . . .
10.14	Lease Agreement. . . .
10.15	Lease Agreement. . . .
10.16	Weight Watchers Savings Plan. . . .
10.17	Weight Watchers Executive Profit Sharing Plan. . . .
10.18	1999 Stock Purchase and Option Plan. . . .
10.19	Weight Watchers Common Stock Incentive Plan. . . .
10.20**	Warrant Agreement. . . .
10.21**	Warrant Certificate of WeightWatchers.com, Inc.. . . .
10.22	Warrant Agreement. . . .
10.23	Warrant Certificate of WeightWatchers.com, Inc. No. 2. . . .
10.24**	Second Amended and Restated Note. . . .
10.25	Warrant Agreement. . . .
10.26	Warrant Certificate of WeightWatchers.com, Inc., No. 3. . . .
10.27	Put/Call Agreement . . . between Weight Watchers International, Inc. and H.J. Heinz Company. . . .
10.28**	Amendment No. 1 to Credit Agreement. . . .
10.29**	Warrant Agreement. . . .
10.30**	Warrant Certificate of WeightWatchers.com, Inc., No. 4. . . .
10.31**	Second Amended and Restated Collateral Assignment and Security Agreement. . . .
10.32**	Termination Agreement . . . between Weight Watchers International, Inc. and Artal Luxembourg
10.33**	Amended and Restated Co-Pack Agreement . . . between Weight Watchers International, Inc. and Nellson Nutraceutical, Inc.
10.34**	Amended and Restated Intellectual Property License Agreement . . . between Weight Watchers International, Inc. and WeightWatchers.com, Inc.
10.35**	Service Agreement . . . between Weight Watchers International, Inc. and WeightWatchers.com, Inc.
10.36**	Corporate Agreement . . . between Weight Watchers International, Inc. and Artal Luxembourg S.A.
10.37**	Guaranty of Sublease. . . .
10.38**	Registration Rights Agreement . . . among Weight Watchers International, Inc., H.J. Heinz Company and Artal Luxembourg S.A.
21**	List of Subsidiaries.
23.1**	Consent of Hunton & Williams (included in Exhibit 5.1).
23.2*	Consent of PricewaterhouseCoopers LLP
23.3*	Consent of PricewaterhouseCoopers LLP
24**	Power of Attorney.

(B) FINANCIAL STATEMENT SCHEDULE

Schedule II — Valuation and Qualifying Accounts — Period from December 30, 2000, and years ended December 30, 2000, April 23, 2000 and April 24, 1999 on page II-7.

REPORT OF INDEPENDENT ACCOUNTANTS
ON FINANCIAL STATEMENT SCHEDULE

To the Board of Directors of Weight Watchers International, Inc.:

Our audits of the consolidated financial statements referred to in our report dated March 2, 2001, except as to Note 21, which is as of November 14, 2001, appearing elsewhere in this Registration Statement also included an audit of the financial statement schedule listed in Item 16(b) of this Form S-1. In our opinion, this financial statement schedule presents fairly, in all material respects, the information set forth therein when read in conjunction with the related consolidated financial statements.

PricewaterhouseCoopers LLP
New York, New York
March 2, 2001

II-6

WEIGHT WATCHERS INTERNATIONAL, INC.
SCHEDULE II—VALUATION AND QUALIFYING ACCOUNTS

[Schedule Omitted:eds.]

ITEM 17. UNDERTAKINGS.

Insofar as indemnification for liabilities arising under the Securities Act of 1933 (the "Securities Act") may be permitted to directors, officers and controlling persons of the registrant pursuant to the foregoing provisions, or otherwise, the registrant has been advised that in the opinion of the Securities and Exchange Commission such indemnification is against public policy as expressed in the Securities Act and is, therefore, unenforceable. In the event that a claim for indemnification against such liabilities (other than the payment by the registrant of expenses incurred or paid by a director, officer or controlling person of the registrant in the successful defense of any action, suit or proceeding) is asserted by such director, officer or controlling person in connection with the securities being registered, the registrant will, unless in the opinion of its counsel the matter has been settled by controlling precedent, submit to a court of appropriate jurisdiction the question whether such indemnification by it is against public policy as expressed in the Securities Act and will be governed by the final adjudication of such issue.

The undersigned registrant hereby undertakes that:

(1) For purposes of determining any liability under the Securities Act, the information omitted from the form of prospectus filed as part of this Registration Statement in reliance upon Rule 430A and contained in a form of prospectus filed by the registrant pursuant to Rule 424(b)(1) or

(4) or 497(h) under the Securities Act shall be deemed to be part of this Registration Statement as of the time it was declared effective.

(2) For the purpose of determining any liability under the Securities Act, each post-effective amendment that contains a form of prospectus shall be deemed to be a new registration statement relating to the securities offered therein, and the offering of such securities at that time shall be deemed to be the initial bona fide offering thereof.

SIGNATURES

Pursuant to the requirements of the Securities Act, the registrant has duly caused this Amendment No. 3 to the Registration Statement to be signed on its behalf by the undersigned, thereunto duly authorized on November 14, 2001.

WEIGHT WATCHERS INTERNATIONAL, INC.
By: *
_____

Linda Huett
President, Chief Executive Officer and
Director

Pursuant to the requirements of the Securities Act, as amended, this Amendment No. 3 to the Registration Statement has been signed below by the following persons in the capacities indicated on the 14th day of November, 2001.

SIGNATURE	TITLE
* ——————————————— Linda Huett	President, Chief Executive Officer and Director
* ——————————————— Thomas S. Kiritsis	Vice President and Chief Financial Officer
* ——————————————— Raymond Debbane	Chairman of the Board of Directors
* ——————————————— Sacha Lainovic	Director

———————————————— Director
              *
    Christopher J. Sobecki

———————————————— Director
              *
    Jonas M. Fajgenbaum

By: **/s/ SACHA LAINOVIC**
       ATTORNEY-IN-FACT

‖ ‖

Rule 424(b)(1) Prospectus Filed by Weight Watchers International, Inc.

FILED PURSUANT TO RULE 424(b)(1)
REGISTRATION NO. 333-69362

17,400,000 Shares

[LOGO]
Common Stock

The shares of common stock are being sold by the selling shareholders named in this prospectus. We will not receive any of the proceeds from the shares of common stock sold by the selling shareholders.

Prior to this offering, there has been no public market for our common stock. Our common stock has been authorized for listing on the New York Stock Exchange under the symbol "WTW."

The underwriters have an option to purchase a maximum of 2,610,000 additional shares from certain of the selling shareholders to cover over-allotments of shares.

Investing in our common stock involves risks. See "Risk Factors" beginning on page 8.

	Price to Public	Underwriting Discounts and Commissions	Proceeds to Selling Shareholders
Per Share	$24.00	$1.26	$22.74
Total	$417,600,000	$21,924,000	$395,676,000

Delivery of the shares of common stock will be made on or about November 20, 2001.

UNDERWRITING

Under the terms and subject to the conditions contained in an underwriting agreement dated November 14, 2001, the selling shareholders have agreed to sell to the underwriters named below, for whom Credit Suisse First Boston Corporation and Goldman, Sachs & Co. are acting as representatives, the following respective numbers of shares of common stock:

UNDERWRITER	NUMBER OF SHARES
Credit Suisse First Boston Corporation	3,809,750
Goldman, Sachs & Co.	3,809,750
Merrill Lynch, Pierce, Fenner & Smith Incorporated	2,643,500
Salomon Smith Barney Inc.	2,643,500
UBS Warburg LLC	2,643,500
ABN AMRO Rothschild LLC	100,000
Banc of America Securities LLC	100,000
Bear, Stearns & Co. Inc.	100,000
Deutsche Banc Alex. Brown Inc.	100,000
A.G. Edwards & Sons, Inc.	100,000
Invemed Associates LLC	100,000
Lehman Brothers Inc.	100,000
J.P. Morgan Securities Inc.	100,000
Prudential Securities Incorporated	100,000
RBC Dain Rauscher Inc.	100,000
Scotia Capital (USA) Inc.	100,000
U.S. Bancorp Piper Jaffray Inc.	100,000
Robert W. Baird & Co. Incorporated	50,000
Davenport & Company LLC	50,000
Gruntal & Co., LLC	50,000
Janney Montgomery Scott LLC	50,000
Johnston, Lemon & Co. Incorporated	50,000
Edward D. Jones & Co., L.P.	50,000
C.L. King & Associates, Inc.	50,000
Legg Mason Wood Walker, Incorporated	50,000
Parker/Hunter Incorporated	50,000
Raymond James & Associates, Inc.	50,000
Sanders Morris Harris	50,000
SunTrust Capital Markets, Inc.	50,000
The Williams Capital Group, L.P.	50,000
Total	$17,400,000

Certain of the selling shareholders have granted to the underwriters a 30-day option to purchase on a pro rata basis up to an aggregate of 2,610,000 additional shares at the initial public offering price less the underwriting discounts and commissions. The option may be exercised only to cover any over-allotments of common stock.

The underwriters propose to offer the shares of common stock initially at the public offering price on the cover page of this prospectus and to selling group members at that price less a selling concession of $0.756 per share. The underwriters and selling group members may allow a discount of $0.10 per share on sales to other broker/dealers. After the initial public offering the representatives may change the public offering price and concession and discount to broker/dealers.

The following table summarizes the compensation the selling shareholders will pay and the estimated expenses we will pay:

		PER SHARE	TOTAL
WITHOUT OVER-ALLOTMENT	WITH OVER-ALLOTMENT	WITHOUT OVER-ALLOTMENT	WITH OVER-ALLOTMENT
Underwriting discounts and commissions paid by selling shareholders			
$1.26	$1.26	$21,924,000	$25,212,600
Expenses payable by us			
$0.12	$0.11	$ 2,230.563	$ 2,250.563

The representatives have informed us that the underwriters do not expect discretionary sales to exceed 5% of the shares of common stock being offered.